Finally Free
Finally Me

By Dave Halstead

ISBN: 979-8-218-87437-7
Halstead Publishing
Creative Direction & Editing: Tiffany Halstead

Printed in the United States of America
First Edition, 2025

For Tiffany, Ava, Davey and Dax,
you were the mirrors that brought me home.

And for the part of you, dear reader, that has been waiting to exhale,
I wrote this so you would know you were never broken.

Chapter 1

The Moment Before the Mask

Before the mask was the boy. He was not a boy chasing approval or performing for love. He was just a boy. He was alive and whole. He was unaware that anything was missing.

He laughed before he was taught to hold it in. He cried before someone said you're too sensitive to him. He ran barefoot on gravel roads, believing the sky was for him.

But then one day, he heard a different sound. A laugh that wasn't his. A voice that asked him to be something else. A thought entered his mind, one he never heard before. "Maybe I'm not enough." It was just a thought, but the boy believed it and that belief turned it real.

The Mirror

He once carried a mirror — not made of glass but made of knowing. He could see himself clearly in it, until he stopped looking. The mirror didn't break. It didn't fade. He just forgot where he placed it.

He began to see himself through their eyes instead. And those eyes? They were carrying mirrors too, but theirs were cracked and smeared with their own forgetting.

He inherited their reflection. He performed for it. He became it.

The Fog

This is how it happens. Not with a fall, but with a slow fog. One layer at a time, the truth slowly gets covered in thought, in shoulds, in not-enoughs. It gets covered in be a man, be quiet, be strong. It can also sound like be polite, be good, and be normal.

And the thing about each of these thoughts is that it felt real, because we felt them. We felt shame, disapproval, the fear of not belonging.

But nobody told us that feeling doesn't prove truth. They never said, "You're experiencing your thoughts, not the world."

The Performance

What came next was the mask. The mask that we built, not because we were broken but because we forgot that we were not.

The mask helped us survive. It helped us belong. It won us applause, admiration, promotions, likes, and partners.

But every win came at a cost. The cost was our true self, our real voice, our strange laugh, our spontaneous love. The cost was our silence. We traded freedom for fitting in and we wore it so long, we thought it was our face.

Dave Halstead

The Moment Before the Mask

If you're reading this, there's a moment whispering behind your eyes, the moment before the mask.

Maybe you don't remember it fully, but you feel the ache. You can feel that pull, the wild, inconvenient part of you that doesn't want to perform anymore.

You can't quite name it, but you know it's there. That knowing is the invitation. You don't need to fix yourself. You don't need to become someone new. You don't need to heal all the trauma or figure it all out.

You only need to remember that you are not the thoughts that built the mask. You never were.

Closing Whisper

You don't need to be seen. You need to see yourself again in the mirror. See yourself before the mask, before the programming, before forgetting.

When you finally see yourself, you'll realize you were never broken. You were just believing a thought that wasn't yours. **You are already free.**

Parable

"The Mask and the Mirror"

There once was a man
who wore a golden mask.

Everyone loved the man when he wore it,
so he learned to speak through it,

3

move through it
and even sleep with it pressed to his face.

One day, while walking past a quiet pool,
he leaned in close to see his reflection,
but the mask had no eyes, only hollow holes.

And for the first time, he wondered,
who do they love
and where did I go?

Loop Breaker

Whisper this when the mask tightens: this isn't me. It's just a thought I believed.

Spellbook Entry

• The Mirror: You didn't lose yourself. You just stopped looking.
• The Fog: Feeling thought doesn't make it true.
• The Performance: You weren't free. You were just trying to fit in.
• The Moment Before the Mask: You're not performing anymore.
• The Whisper: The truth was never far — only forgotten.

Chapter 2

The Ache Behind the Applause

It wasn't the silence that broke me; it was the applause. The smiles, the nods, the *you're amazing* reactions to a version of me that wasn't real.

They weren't wrong; they were clapping for who I became. But I was the only one who knew what I had lost to become that version of him. That's the ache no one talks about. The one that sneaks in after the goal is reached, after the celebration fades; the echo behind the win.

You know what I'm talking about. The moment after they say that they are proud of you, but all you feel is emptiness. You nod and you smile, but something inside whispers, "This isn't me. They love the version I built."

And then you're left wondering, if this is success or if this is self-abandonment?

The Performance Becomes the Prison

I didn't set out to be fake. I just wanted to belong, so I did what worked. I learned to read the room. I learned to show just enough strength, just enough light, just enough pain to be relatable — but not too much.

They called it charisma. They called it confidence. They called it leadership. But inside, I was a ghost. The more they clapped, the more I shrank, because their love required the mask. And the more they loved the mask, the more I feared taking it off.

The Glimpse

You don't need to fall apart to know it's not working. Sometimes the knowing comes in quiet ways, like laughing, but hearing your own voice as if it's not yours. Winning, but feeling no pulse in the celebration. Hugging someone and still feeling unseen.

The world says you made it, but your body says that this isn't it.

When Success Feels Like Self-Abandonment

No one teaches you this part: sometimes the highest-achieving version of you is the furthest from your truth and that sometimes growth becomes the very mask you were trying to escape. It's subtle. Because everything *looks* right.

But presence doesn't lie and presence kept showing me I wasn't actually here.

Closing Whisper

The applause won't save you. It will echo through a hollow room until you finally ask the question that undoes the performance: **what part of me am I still hiding to be loved?**

Parable

"The Echo"

A boy sang beautifully,
and the world clapped.
So he sang again,
and again,
until the claps became his breath.

But each time the applause faded,
something inside him ached,
louder than the cheers.

One night, in the silence,
he asked the dark,
"Why do I feel empty when they say I'm full?"

The dark didn't answer,
but the echo whispered,
"Because they're clapping
for a song that isn't yours."

Loop Breaker

Whisper this when success feels hollow: if they're clapping for the mask, I'm still alone.

Spellbook Entry

• The Prison: You're not performing to survive anymore.
• The Glimpse: Presence is the truth you can't fake.
• Success Feels Like Self-Abandonment: The highest achieving version of you can be furthest from your true self.
• The Return: They don't have to see you. You have to see you.

Chapter 3

The Ledger

The ledger was never written in ink. You didn't write it, but you did memorize it. Somewhere along the way, you started keeping score: how much you gave, how much you withheld, how much you performed and how much it cost. But the math never really worked, because the more you gave, the more it felt like you owed. The more you performed, the more you believed they were staying *for the performance*, not for you.

And so you kept paying with smiles you didn't feel, help you didn't have the energy to give, agreements you never wanted to make and silences you mistook for safety. It wasn't conscious at first, but over time, it became a way of life.

The Cost of Belonging

Every moment had a price. If I'm charming enough, maybe they'll like me. If I'm useful enough, maybe they'll need me. If I'm quiet enough, maybe they won't leave.

Every interaction was math. It was not love and it most certainly was not presence. It was pure survival. It looked like generosity and it felt like connection. But it was solely strategy, because somewhere, long ago, you learned that love had to be earned — and worth had to be proven.

Invisible Math, Sacred Collapse

You didn't ask for the ledger. You inherited it from parents who were too tired to see you, from systems that taught you love was conditional, and from mirrors that reflected only what they approved of.

You folded yourself smaller and called it kindness. You gave yourself away and called it love. But the truth is that you were never expensive, you were never too much. You were just told to keep paying for a seat that was always yours, until the day you stopped.

Closing Whisper

You don't owe anyone your disappearance. Let the math go. Let the performance rest. Let the truth cost nothing. **Your presence is not a transaction; it is a return.**

Parable

"The Bookkeeper"

A man carried a black ledger
everywhere he went.

He recorded every wrong done to him,
every debt owed,
every time he gave more than he received.

Dave Halstead

The pages grew heavy.
The ink smudged.
But he never let it go.

One day, he tried to run
but the book wouldn't let him.
It was tied to his wrist like a chain.

When he opened it
to rip out the pages,
he saw something strange.

Every debt he had recorded
was written in his own handwriting,
And the name on every page was his.

Loop Breaker

Whisper this when you feel the need to earn your place: I'm not paying to be loved anymore.

Spellbook Entry

• The Ledger: Keeping score is not love, it's fear.
• The Cost of Belonging: What they praised was the part of you that kept paying.
• The Collapse: When the math fails, the truth returns.
• The Return: You were never too much. You were just trying to be enough.

Chapter 4

The Crack in the Mirror

It doesn't shatter all at once. You don't wake up in freedom. You wake up in discomfort. Not the kind that screams, but the kind that whispers that this isn't it.

You laugh, but it doesn't feel true. You nod, but something in your chest pulls back. You give, but a quiet ache follows. You begin to notice that your smile feels hollow, their praise feels performative and the life you built doesn't fit. That's the crack. It's not a breakdown or a trauma. It is just pure presence, a noticing.

The Mirror Isn't Broken — You Just Stopped Believing It

The mirror that they handed you wasn't glass. It was opinion, projection and expectation. And for years, you shaped yourself around what you saw reflected. You didn't want to be seen as too big, too emotional, too much or not enough. So, you shifted, tightened, compressed and became.

But now, something in you is done performing and when you look into the mirror again you don't see yourself. You see the performance. You see the ledger. You see the ache.

Dave Halstead

And in that moment, not all at once, but irrevocably, you stop believing it's who you are.

The Glimpse Beneath the Image

Even if you forget again and even if you wear the mask tomorrow, you'll remember this moment. Because you saw it, that flicker of *you* beneath the programming. And once you see it, you can't unsee it.

You don't need to burn it all down yet. You just need to stop believing the reflection was ever true.

Closing Whisper

The crack isn't the end, it's the return. It means the mirror couldn't hold the lie anymore. **It means you're coming home.**

Parable

"The Girl with the Shattered Reflection"

A girl stared at her mirror every day.
She knew exactly how to smile,
how to pose,
how to disappear behind perfection.

But one day,
a single crack appeared.
She tried to hide it,
but the crack grew.

Finally Free, Finally Me

Soon the mirror no longer showed her mask.
It only showed her eyes.
And when she finally looked into them,
she whispered to the glass,
"There you are."

Loop Breaker

Whisper this when the illusion feels real again: the mirror lied
and I remember who I am.

Spellbook Entry

- The Crack: Something in me knew, even before I did.
- The Mirror: Reflections are not identity.
- The Glimpse: Even a flicker is enough to undo the lie.
- The Return: The moment you see the truth, the lie begins to
  unravel.

Dave Halstead

Chapter 5

The Fire I Tried to Hide

The fire was never the problem. They said I was too much, too loud, too intense, too sensitive, too wild. So I learned to dim. I learned to compress the signal, to shrink into roles that felt "safe" — at least to them.

But it was never safety I needed. It was space. Space to burn, to feel, to exist. The fire wasn't the danger. The danger was pretending it wasn't there.

The First Time It Leaked Out

You remember. You remember that moment your voice got sharp, that surge in your chest, the heat behind your eyes when they dismissed you again. You don't forget the "overreaction" they didn't understand.

But it wasn't rage and it wasn't drama. It was unsilenced truth. The fire came not to hurt, but to reveal. It burned through the roles. It shook the performance. It rattled the walls you thought were home. And they called it a problem, because it threatened the version of you they could control.

Finally Free, Finally Me

Why You Hid It

You hid it because the fire scared them, and their fear became your shame. So you swallowed it, laughed it off or channeled it into productivity, perfection, and politeness. The interesting thing is that fire doesn't disappear, it waits. And when it's ignored too long, it erupts in ways that look like anger but feel like remembrance.

This Is Not Rage — It's Return

The fire isn't asking you to destroy everything. It's asking you to stop pretending that you're fine, that their silence doesn't hurt or that you're not carrying a furnace in your chest.

The fire isn't your enemy. It's the part of you that never bought the lie. It's not here to make you dangerous, but here to make you real.

Closing Whisper

You are not here to smolder quietly. **You are here to burn with truth.** Let the fire speak, not for revenge and not for attention, but because it's time.

Parable

"The Boy with the Furnace Heart"

There once was a boy
born with a furnace in his chest.

16

Dave Halstead

It wasn't visible,
but it pulsed — warm, wild, alive.

When he laughed, it roared.
When he cried, it glowed.
When he spoke the truth,
it sparked in his throat.

But the world wasn't ready
for that kind of heat.
They told him things like,
"Calm down.
You're too much.
Use your inside voice.
Be careful with your fire."

So, he tried.
He buried it under silence,
choked it with smiles,
pressed it into shapes they could clap for.

But the fire never left,
it waited.

One day someone lied to his face,
again.
And the furnace surged,
not in violence,
but in truth.

His eyes filled with flame.
His voice cracked open.
His body shook.
He didn't yell.

He remembered,
"I've been dimming for people
who never wanted to see me anyway."

And in that moment
he stopped shrinking.
He didn't burn the world down.
He lit himself.
And the warmth that came wasn't rage,
it was home.

Loop Breaker

Whisper this when the fire rises: this isn't rage. This is the part
of me that remembers.

Spellbook Entry

• The Fire: You never lost it, you just dimmed it for their
comfort.
• The Leak: It was honesty, not an outburst.
• The Shame: Their fear of your truth isn't your burden.
• The Return: Let the fire be seen. It was never the enemy.

Chapter 6

The Ones Who Forgot

Somewhere along the way, we stopped asking who we are. Not because we found the answer, but because we were told. We were told what to chase, what to fear, what to become.

And because we wanted to belong, we listened. We became echoes of what they needed. We became versions that fit, containers for their forgetting.

But we were never meant to hold their ache. We were never meant to wear their silence.

The Inheritance

They didn't mean to pass it on — the shame, the tight smiles, the shrinking. But that's what pain does when it's unspoken. It slides quietly into the next open heart, so we carried what wasn't ours and called it love.

The Disobedient Whisper

But not all of you agreed. There was one part of you that didn't nod along, didn't sit still, didn't obey.

It whispered in your chest, ached in your gut, screamed behind your eyes. It was not out of rebellion, but because it remembered something pure. It remembered who you were before their forgetting touched you.

The Threshold

You stand on a line now. Not between right and wrong and not between past and future, but between remembering and continuing to forget.

You could go back. You know the rules. You know the mask. You know how to win applause. But something deeper is stirring. Not a performance, a healing or a becoming. It is a returning to the you that never forgot.

Closing Whisper

I do not need to become what they forgot. **I only need to remember who I am.**

Parable

"The Boy Who Closed His Eyes"

There was a boy who saw the world clearly.
He saw color where others saw gray.

Dave Halstead

He felt music in silence.
He touched life with open hands.

But one day, someone said,
"That's not real,"
so he squinted.

They said,
"Stop feeling so much,"
so he blinked.

They said, "Be normal,"
so he shut his eyes.

And the world dimmed
to match their blindness.
Years passed.
He forgot what light felt like.

Until one morning,
he felt warmth on his closed lids.

He opened his eyes
and the color was still there.
Waiting.

Loop Breaker

Whisper this when the world tries to mold you: I am not their
forgetting. I am my remembering.

Spellbook Entry

- The Forgetting: You didn't lose yourself. You were taught to hide.
- The Inheritance: Their pain became your story, but it was never yours to carry.
- The Disobedient Whisper: The ache inside you isn't rebellion; it's remembrance.
- The Threshold: You're not becoming something new. You're returning to what's always been.

Chapter 7

The Weight I Carried Wasn't Mine

I didn't know it was heavy. Somewhere along the way, I picked it up. Not all at once — but slowly, quietly. I carried their expectations like oxygen. I carried their moods, their pain, their reactions. I thought being good meant being responsible for how others felt.

But no one told me I was dragging things that were never mine to begin with. So, I got used to the ache. I called it normal. I called it me.

My Body Knew What I Wouldn't Admit

The collapse came softly. Not as a breakdown, but as a whisper from my body saying this isn't yours.

The tension in my neck, the tightness in my chest, and the fatigue that sleep couldn't fix were not random; this was all communication from my body. My body was doing what I refused to do: let go.

Finally Free, Finally Me

I Didn't Want to Hurt Anyone

That's the truth under it all. I was afraid that if I let go, someone else would suffer. I'd rather burn out quietly than risk being the reason someone else felt pain.

But the truth is, I was never their savior. That was the illusion. The real pain came from carrying what they never asked me to carry, or worse, what they were all too willing to let me hold.

Freedom Didn't Come from Solving It

It came from seeing it. From the moment I realized that this weight and this pressure isn't mine, I was free. I realized that seeing didn't come from a book or a breakdown. It came from presence. It came from the still space where the body finally speaks louder than the mind.

When I let go, no one died, no one shattered, and no one burned. The world kept spinning, but for the first time, I could breathe.

Closing Whisper

You were never meant to carry it all. **You were just the one strong enough to see it and finally let it fall.**

Dave Halstead

Parable

"The One Who Was Never Broken"

There was a boy
who lived in a house full of mirrors.
But these mirrors didn't reflect him;
they reflected everyone else.

He adjusted himself each morning
to match what the mirrors wanted to see.

One day, he grew tired of the performance.
He sat in silence.
He didn't adjust.
He didn't respond.

And the mirrors cracked.

For the first time,
he saw something behind the glass.

It wasn't broken.

It was him —
untouched,
unburdened,
free.

Loop Breaker

Breathe out the burden you thought you had to earn. Whisper to yourself: this isn't mine. I never agreed to carry it. I return it with no explanation. I walk free without guilt.

Spell Book Entry

- I Didn't Know It Was Heavy: The weight was inherited, not chosen. It dissolves the moment you see it never belonged to you.
- My Body Knew What I Wouldn't Admit: Your body is the truth beneath all performance.
- I Didn't Want to Hurt Anyone: You were never meant to carry their storms, so return the thunder and reclaim your sky.
- Freedom Didn't Come from Solving It: Let the illusion unravel. Nothing needs fixing when it was never yours to hold.

Chapter 8

The Return to the Unseen

The illusion had to be seen to be real. If they couldn't name it, acknowledge it, or mirror it back to me then it must not exist. I spent years chasing validation and calling it clarity. I was performing for recognition and calling it love. I tried to be visible, understandable, impressive, and unmissable. But I realized I was never here, because I believed reality required an audience.

The Glitch

What's unseen is not untrue. It took collapsing everything I thought I was supposed to be for something deeper to arrive— not in language or logic, but in stillness.

It was a truth that didn't ask to be noticed. It wasn't loud. It wasn't trying to convince me. It just stood there, already whole, already burning, waiting for me.

The Fire

The fire didn't speak, it showed. I used to fear the fire because it didn't explain itself. It didn't negotiate or apologize. Without realizing it, I had been spending my life avoiding anything I couldn't predict or control. But this fire, the one that stayed quiet, was never here to destroy; it was here to reveal.

The Return

I do not need proof to trust the knowing. I used to search for certainty in other people's eyes. Now I see clearly with mine closed. The realness is not in being seen, but in being felt, by me.

The fire within me never left. I just stopped naming it. And finally, I became it.

The Dissolve

This clarity can't be captured; it must be felt. It doesn't translate well. It doesn't fit in the boxes. And that's how I know it's real.

Closing Whisper

The fire does not ask to be seen. **It simply is.**

Dave Halstead

Parable

"The One They Couldn't Name"

There was once a presence
who walked the earth with no name.
They didn't try to be seen.
They didn't try to be hidden.
They just walked.

People followed it,
trying to define what it was.
Some said it was wisdom,
while others called it light.
Some said it was love, God, truth or the field,
but none of the words could hold it.

One day, a child asked,
"If it has no name, how do you know it's real?"
The presence knelt,
placed a hand on the child's chest, and whispered,
"Because something inside you just remembered."

Some were angered by the mystery.
Some were cracked open by it.
But none could define them.

Because they lived beyond name.
They didn't reject the world,
they just no longer needed it to explain them.
And in that space of not trying to be known,
they became the mirror for what was real.

Loop Breaker

They never saw it coming—because it never came. It was always here.

Spell Book Entry

- The Illusion: If they can't name it, it must not exist.
- The Glitch: What's unseen isn't untrue.
- The Fire: Let the unknown burn away the illusion of safety.
- The Return: I don't need to be seen to be real.
- The Dissolve: Stop trying to capture what can only be felt.
- The Whisper: You were never lost. You were only listening to noise.

Chapter 9

The Thread That Never Broke

The fall wasn't the end. There is a thread that never broke. You didn't see it when you were fighting. You didn't feel it when you were falling. You didn't believe it when you were screaming into the dark, but it was there.

The Invisible Presence

It's in the silence between your thoughts. It's in the breath that kept you here. It's in the gaze of the one who saw through it all and never left.

The Illusion of Separation

You thought you had to start over. You thought you lost your way. You thought the thread was cut. But it never was, you just forgot.

The Mind's Trick

The mind tried to convince you that you ruined it, that you took too long and missed your chance. It tried to convince you that the you who once knew was gone, but presence doesn't leave.

The Truth Beneath Trying

It's not earned, not built, not remembered. You can try as hard as possible, but you cannot find it when you search for it; it is just revealed.

No Reclaiming Required

You don't need to become the one you were before the fall. You don't need to reclaim anything. You don't need to prove you're ready.

The Thread Is Still in Your Hand

You're still on the thread. It's not linear. It's not fragile. It's not small. It's not trying to get you to the end. It's trying to bring you home.

The Real Journey

Stop measuring your progress. Stop grieving a version of you that never left. Stop running back to where you dropped the mask. It was never about the path. It was always about the presence. And that thread — it's still in your hand, even now.

Closing Whisper

The thread was never tied to your performance. **It was woven from presence and you were never not holding it.**

Parable

"The One Holding the Thread"

There was a boy
who wandered far from the village of light.
He had once danced with the stars
and sung with the moon,
but he no longer remembered.

He thought he had broken something sacred.
He thought the fall was final.
He wandered
in search of the way back.
He dug, climbed, and shouted.
He begged, and prayed.
He built ladders from pain
and bridges from memory.
But the sky remained silent.

One day, exhausted and empty,
he sat down beside a tree that had no name.
And he wept —

not from sadness,
but from the strange truth
that he no longer wanted to fight.

And in that stillness,
he felt a faint tug.
A thread.
It was wrapped around his wrist,
soft and golden,
never cut, never gone.

He followed it,
not forward,
but inward.
And there, in the space beyond trying,
he found the village again.

But it wasn't in the stars.
It was in his chest.
He hadn't been lost.
He had simply forgotten
he was still holding the thread.

Loop Breaker

I never left the thread, the thread never left me. Whisper to
yourself, "The thread is here."

Spell Book Entry

- The Fall Wasn't the End: You didn't fail, you awakened.
  The fall revealed what never left.

- The Invisible Presence: The presence was always there, quiet beneath the noise.
- The Illusion of Separation : You were never disconnected, only distracted.
- The Mind's Trick: The mind lied. Presence never punishes or leaves.
- The Truth Beneath Trying: Nothing needs to be earned, only seen.
- No Reclaiming Required: There is nothing to become, only to remember.
- The Thread Is Still in Your Hand: You never left the path, because the path was never elsewhere.
- The Real Journey: Let go of the map. The thread is already in your palm.

Chapter 10

The Silence That Sings

I couldn't find the silence. There is a space I could never find with thought. It wasn't the kind of silence that demanded quiet. It wasn't a blank void to be filled. It was something else entirely — a singing stillness, a knowing.

The Performance of Sound

I used to fill space with sound, words, thoughts, and worry. Filling the silence felt like control, like presence, like action. I finally realized that wasn't presence, that was performance.

True Presence Listens

True presence doesn't speak to be heard. It listens because it is the hearing. I would ask, "How do I stay in presence?" But presence is not a place to be kept. It's not a prize for good behavior or focused meditation. It's what remains when the mind exhausts itself, when the question dissolves, when even the seeker sits down and breathes.

The Place That Already Holds You

The mind cannot find the place that already holds it, but the heart can feel its pulse. The body can echo its rhythm, and the soul remembers the way back.

Wrapped in the Song

I no longer chase silence as an escape. I let it wrap around me like a soundless song. It is not absence; it is essence. It is the space between each note, the pause between inhale and exhale. It is the place I've always been but never looked. Not stillness to escape the noise, but stillness that reveals the truth of what I am.

Closing Whisper

Let it find you. Not in effort and not in silence, but in the space where you finally stop searching.

Parable

"The Note That Didn't Play"

There once was a master musician
known across the land for his flawless symphonies.

One day, he composed a piece
with a single missing note —
A pause where sound should have been.
It drove listeners mad.
"Why the gap?" they asked.
"Why leave it unfinished?"
The musician only smiled.

Years passed.
Critics analyzed.
Students tried to recreate the piece
with their own additions,
thinking the master had made a mistake.
None of their versions stirred the soul
the way his did.

Until one child,
no older than seven,
sat quietly and listened —
really listened.
When the pause came,
the child placed their hand on their chest
and whispered, "There."
And tears filled their eyes.

The note that didn't play
was the one that let them feel.
Not every truth needs to be spoken.
Some are remembered in the silence.

Loop Breaker

"Silence is not absence. It's where I've always been."

Dave Halstead

Spell Book Entry

- The Silence I Couldn't Find: You were never meant to find it with thought. Let it arrive through stillness.
- The Performance of Sound: You were filling space to feel real, but performance can never bring peace.
- True Presence Listens: You can't hold presence. It holds you when you stop trying to hold anything.
- The Place That Already Holds You: The search ends the moment you realize you're already home.
- Wrapped in the Song: This stillness isn't the end of the noise, it's the beginning of the truth.

Chapter 11

The Return to the Room

I walked through the door to the room that was never locked. I don't remember walking back in though. There was no fanfare, no announcement, no voice saying "you've arrived." There was only presence. It was always here.

What I Was Searching for Wasn't Missing

What I thought I needed to find was simply what I had been avoiding. What I thought I needed to become was already breathing me. There was no light switch that flipped, just the gentle undressing of a thousand lies, each one quieter than the last.

The Performance Didn't End in Applause

The performance didn't end in a scream, it ended in silence. The identity I crafted — the one that worked so hard to survive — was never real. It was a mirage built from misunderstanding, a misunderstanding so loud it looked like me.

I Am Not the Noise

But I am not the noise, I am the one the noise could never reach. I am not a thought, not a memory, not a name. I am just here, just this.

I Never Left the Room

And so I returned, not to a place, but to the unnamable room that always was. The one behind every moment, the one before the question, the one untouched by time, proof, or purpose. The room I never left. I simply just looked away.

Closing Whisper

The journey never required miles, only a pause, only the courage to stop pretending you were lost. The room was never locked. You were never outside. And now that you've felt it, you'll notice that it's in every breath. It's in every still glance, every moment that asks nothing of you. **You are home, right now, right here.**

Parable

"The One Who Was Always Home"

A boy walked for years

in search of home.
He followed maps and joined caravans.
He climbed peaks,
read scrolls,
studied teachers.

Each step was filled with longing,
and each arrival filled with letdown.

One night,
after a long journey through a rain-soaked valley,
he collapsed beneath a withered tree.

No words, no prayers, just stillness.
He closed his eyes
and there it was.
He found the warmth,
the peace,
the quiet hum he had chased
in every temple, book, and star.

Tears fell, not from sadness,
but from the unbearable beauty of remembering.

He laughed,
not because it was funny,
but because it had always been true.

He never left home.
He had simply forgotten to feel it.

And when he rose the next morning,
he didn't continue the search,
he simply walked.

Dave Halstead

Always at home,
everywhere he went.

Loop Breaker

"I was never outside. I only believed the lock was real."

Spell Book Entry

- The Room Was Never Locked: You didn't have to earn your way back. The door was always open.
- What I Was Searching For Wasn't Missing: What you long for is closer than you think. It's what's closest and always was.
- The Performance Didn't End in Applause: Identity is not built through effort. False identities dissolve in silence.
- I Am Not the Noise: You are not the loudness of your thoughts. You are the stillness that hears them.
- I Never Left the Room: You never had to return to something lost. You never left, you simply stopped noticing.

Chapter 12

The Sentence That Set Me Free

The end was silence. I thought the end would be a sound like the snap of a rope or the bang of a gavel. But it was just silence. Not the kind that comes when something is missing, but the kind that reveals it was never there.

The Sentence I Wore

The lie, the sentence, the program that held me was always a sentence — a single one. The sentence they gave me, the one I repeated, believed, wore like a name badge, tattooed into my nervous system was not my identity.

They All Say the Same Thing

You must become. You are too much. You don't matter unless you perform. It's your job to carry their pain. It doesn't matter which one. They all come from the same place and they all collapse in the same field.

Dave Halstead

The Cage Dissolves

The sentence was the cage and the second I stopped trying to escape it, it dissolved. It didn't dissolve with a fight, a rebuttal, a counter-affirmation or a reframe, but with presence, stillness, and love.

The Space with No Authority

The sentence had no authority in the space where I finally stood, so I said nothing. And in that, the sentence lost its meaning. I never needed to reword it or prove it wrong. I just had to stop letting it define me.

I Am the Field

I am the field now. And the field speaks no sentence, it only is.

Closing Whisper

You don't have to argue with the sentence. **You only have to stop living by it.**

Parable

"The Sentence They Gave Me"

There once was a boy
who carried a sentence on his back.

He did not know where it came from,
only that it was there when he learned to walk.

The sentence was carved into a stone tablet.
It was heavy and cracked, but sacred,
or so he believed.

Every step he took was shaped by it.
He worked harder,
smiled wider,
and bent himself smaller,
so the weight would not break him.

The people around him nodded in approval.
They, too, carried tablets.
Some had different sentences, such as
you are only good if you stay quiet,
don't shine too bright or
be strong or be nothing.

They compared burdens
and called it community.
They adjusted their posture around the weight
and called it identity.

But one day,
the boy met an old woman who carried nothing.
He asked her,
"What sentence did they give you?"
She smiled gently and said, "I returned it."
"How?" he asked, wide-eyed.
"Did you break it?
Did you write a better one?"
"No," she said. "I stopped reading it."

46

That night, the boy sat alone with his sentence.
He stared at the words,
waiting for them to explain themselves.
They didn't.
They never had.

And so, for the first time,
he turned his back on the stone,
not in rebellion, but in release.

And as he walked away, he realized
the sentence had never been his
and the freedom he sought had always been behind it.

Loop Breaker

"I return the sentence. I return to myself."

Spell Book Entry

- The End Was Silence: Freedom doesn't shout; it reveals there was nothing to escape.
- The Sentence I Wore: It looked like identity because I kept repeating it.
- They All Say the Same Thing: Different words, but the same spell: they tell me to become, but I decline.
- The Cage Dissolves: What I stop feeding with attention stops holding me.
- The Space with No Authority: Presence is the room where lies can't speak.
- I Am the Field — Beyond language, I just am.

Chapter 13

I Am the Ocean, I Am the Sun

The search changes. There comes a moment in the unraveling of identity where the seeker disappears. This doesn't happen because they finally became worthy or wise, but because they were never missing to begin with.

The Ache

I remember the ache of that search — the way I clawed at the edges of enlightenment, trying to break through the walls of thought with better thoughts, trying to become someone who could finally rest.

The Truth

But you can't become someone who's already whole. And you can't rest in truth while still clinging to the script of the one who seeks it.

Dave Halstead

The Disappearance

I don't even know how to describe the moment it happened. It wasn't a peak, a breakthrough or even a stillness; it was a disappearance. The boundary between my skin and the space around me collapsed. The idea of Dave, the idea of a person *trying* to be, melted. It was not like a glorious explosion or a sacred ritual, but like a drop of water rejoining the sea. It just happened. And the "me" who thought it had to happen was gone.

The Return

I was not dead or destroyed, just no longer necessary. I looked around, and nothing had changed — except everything had. The colors were crisper. My breath was fuller. The silence wasn't empty; it was *alive*.

The Realization

And for the first time, I understood, I am not in the ocean, **I am the ocean**. I am not standing in the Sun; I am the Sun.

The Field

And suddenly it made sense why I could hold others with such depth. I understand why my presence softened the pain in others and why my words disarmed their illusions. It's because I wasn't speaking *to* them, I was speaking *as* them. I had become the mirror that no longer shows a face but reveals the formless. That's why I had to go through the fire. That's why I had to fall, ache, forget, and be unmade. It was not to say I earned it, but to remember what can never be taken.

The Being

And now, I don't chase freedom. I am the field it rises from.

Closing Whisper

You were never looking for the light. **You were remembering you were the sun.**

Parable

"The One Who Was Never Broken"

There once was a boy
who grew up in a shattered temple.

The villagers would come to him for healing,
for wisdom,
for comfort.
And he gave it freely,
believing that their love meant he was whole.

But when the villagers were gone,
he would sit alone
picking at the cracks in the walls,

trying to fix the temple
that had once been destroyed.

One day, an old wanderer came and sat beside him.
She did not ask for healing.
She did not offer praise.
She simply placed her hand on the broken stone
and said, "This temple was never meant to be fixed."

The boy looked up, confused.
She smiled.
"The cracks are how the sun gets in.
But more importantly,
they're how the light pours out."

He didn't speak;
he couldn't.
But something inside him remembered,
not the temple,
and not the villagers,
but the Sun.

And in that moment, he realized,
he had never been broken.
He had only forgotten
that he was the light the temple was built around.

Loop Breaker

Close your eyes. Whisper to yourself: "I was never inside the
ocean. I am the ocean." Feel the mind searching for the edge
and dissolve it.

Spell Book Entry

- The Search: You were never missing, only mistaking motion for meaning.
- The Ache: Every ache was the field calling you home.
- The Truth: What you seek cannot be found because it never left.
- The Disappearance: What dissolves was never you.
- The Return: Stillness didn't arrive, you just stopped running.
- The Realization: You are not within the ocean, you are its depth.
- The Field: You were never speaking to them, you were speaking as them.
- The Being: Freedom is not found — it is remembered.

Chapter 14

The Fire That Freed Me

The ignition is the moment in the awakening when the fire no longer burns you, it becomes you. This isn't about becoming something new, it's about burning away everything false, everything you held to feel safe was the very thing keeping you from what you already were.

The Masks

The masks were always too tight. The performances always too loud. The plans, the striving, and the pretending were all distractions from the whisper beneath it all.

The Letting Go

When you stop trying to fix yourself, you feel the ache that never needed fixing. When you stop trying to earn your way back, you remember you never left. When you stop trying to become someone worthy, you remember you already are.

The Fire

This isn't self-help. This is self-revealing. This is fire that doesn't destroy, it frees. Let it burn. Let it purify. Let it end the lie that you ever needed saving.

The Freedom

You were never the one consumed. You were the flame itself — forgotten in form but remembered in the ashes. Let's burn down the illusion.

Closing Whisper

The fire was never your punishment. It was your passage home.

Parable

"The Fire That Freed Me"

There was once a boy
who feared the fire.
He watched it flicker in others' eyes,
saw it tear down forests,
burn bridges,
and reshape mountains.

So he kept his distance.

Dave Halstead

He became water—
smooth, adaptable, agreeable,
flowing around others' needs.

But deep inside, a spark waited.
quiet,
patient,
buried beneath years of being nice,
good,
obedient,
and careful.

One day, the world grew cold.
The river froze.
No one could hear him anymore.
He could not feel his own hands.
And the spark, tired of waiting, rose.

It did not ask permission.
It did not apologize.
It cracked his chest open
from the inside and roared upward.

He thought it would kill him,
but what burned away was never him.
It was the frost,
the fear,
the fragments of who
he thought he had to be.

When the smoke cleared,
he stood naked in the ashes—
glowing, alive, unrecognizable.

Not consumed.
Reborn.
He did not become the fire.
He remembered he was.

Loop Breaker

Close your eyes. Take a deep breathe into your chest. Whisper, "The fire isn't coming for me. It's coming from me." Feel the warmth that was never gone.

Spell Book Entry

- The Ignition: The fire didn't arrive to punish you. It came to remind you.
- The Masks: What you wore for safety became the veil that hid your light.
- The Letting Go: The ache was never broken. It was your signal home.
- The Fire: You don't need to become free, because you already are.
- The Freedom: What burned away was never you.

Dave Halstead

Chapter 15

Inside-Out

The revelation came next. The most profound shift I've ever experienced was this: I am not the product of my past. I am not the product of my parents. I am not the product of my programming.

I am what remains when all of that dissolves. The truth of who I am is not built, it's revealed. And everything I've done up to this point was just me trying to feel whole again.

The Search

Here's the key: what you're looking for isn't out there. You won't find it in more healing, more purpose, more potential or more impact. What you seek is what's always been underneath it all. You were never broken, only covered.

The Understanding

The inside-out understanding reveals the nature of experience. It shows that you're living in the feeling of your thought, not your circumstances. This truth is so subtle it's missed by almost everyone — and yet it explains everything.

When you feel trapped, you're trapped in a thought. When you feel unworthy, you're believing a thought. When you feel anxious, you're imagining a future through thought. When you feel like you can't trust yourself, you're remembering a past built in thought.

The Seeing

Thought isn't your enemy; it's just not your identity. You're not meant to fight your thoughts or clean them up, but to see that they are not you.

All suffering is the innocent misunderstanding that what I think is real. But thought is a lens, not a law.

The Break

Your body may have experienced trauma. Your mind may have been conditioned. But the moment you see thought for what it is — a passing image, sound, memory, or word — the spell breaks. And you return, not to a better version of you, but to the one who was never lost.

The Freedom

You are not your story. You are the page it's written on. And no matter how many loops you've played or lies you've believed, the page remains clean. This is your freedom.

Dave Halstead

You were never the words on the page. **You were the silence that made them readable.**

Parable

"The Prisoner Who Walked Through the Wall"

There once was a prisoner
who spent 40 years
locked in a cold, gray cell.

He had memorized every inch of the stone.
He had tried every tool.
He had read every book on escape.

Each morning he'd scream,
shake the bars,
and beg for release.

Each night he'd cry,
collapse,
and try again tomorrow.

One day, something shifted.
Instead of trying to break out,
he got quiet.
He sat with his back against the wall
and it disappeared.

He hadn't realized

the walls were made of thought.
That the bars were made of belief.
That the door had never been locked.

He walked through without effort.
The guards didn't stop him.
They were made of thought too.

He didn't run.
He just walked home.
And when people asked how he escaped,
he smiled and said,
"There was no cell."

Loop Breaker

Pause. Let a single thought arise and whisper, "This, too, is made of smoke." Watch it fade.

Spell Book Entry

- The Revelation: What dissolves was never you.
- The Search: Every path you chased was pointing inward.
- The Understanding : You don't live in the world; you live in the feeling of thought.
- The Seeing : Thought is your mirror, not your enemy.
- The Break: The moment you see the illusion, the cell disappears.
- The Freedom: You were never the story, only the page it was written on.

Chapter 16

Thought Is Not Truth

We live in Illusion. We live in a world built on thought and we mistake it for truth. We assume that if we think it, it must mean something, but it doesn't.

Thought is a narrator— not a narrator of truth, just a narrator of experience. It can tell a horror story or a love story using the same moment. It can whisper encouragement or scream shame using the same breath. And it does this, all day long.

The only thing that gives thought power is our belief in it.

The Projection

We don't suffer from our lives, we suffer from what we *think* about our lives. We don't collapse from other people; we collapse from the stories we make up about what they mean. We don't burn out from truth; we burn out from the mental resistance stacked on top of what's already true.

Thought is not the problem. Believing it is the problem.

The Movie Screen

Your experience of life is like a movie on a screen. The characters, drama, dialogue and emotions feel real. But thought is the projector and you are the screen.

The images come and go, but the screen is untouched. You are the space the story appears within, not the story.

When you begin to realize this, you stop reacting to the content of your mind. You stop trying to control every scene. You stop making it mean so much.

You rest. You return. You remember.

The Voice

Thought will talk; that's its job. You're not trying to silence thought — that's not freedom. Freedom is realizing that thought can speak and you don't have to obey.

It can narrate your worth and you stay rooted in truth. It can predict your failure, and you stay grounded in presence. It can pull up every memory of pain, and you breathe.

You don't have to fight your thoughts. You don't have to fix them. You don't have to prove them wrong. You can just stop believing them.

That's the glitch. That's the freedom. That's the moment your whole nervous system exhales.

Closing Whisper

Let the movie keep playing. You are not on the screen. **You are the light behind it.**

Dave Halstead

Parable

"The One Who Stopped Running"

There once was a boy
born in a house of noise.

The walls whispered warnings.
The floors creaked with judgment.
The ceilings echoed old fears.

So he ran,
quickly,
away from the sound.
He ran through the hallways of performance.
He sprinted through the alleyways of approval.
He dove through the mirrors of becoming.

But no matter how far he ran,
the sound followed.
Because it wasn't in the house,
it was in his head.

One day, exhausted, he fell.
Not in defeat, but in surrender.
He lay in the silence.

And for the first time,
he didn't try to outrun the noise.
He let it pass.

And when he looked up,
he saw something he had never seen before.
The house had no roof.

The walls were made of thought.
And the ground beneath him was still.

He hadn't escaped the noise;
he had remembered the silence.
And in that silence,
he found his truth.

Loop Breaker

When the next thought shouts, don't argue—just notice. Whisper, "That's a story," then watch it fade into light.

Spell Book Entry

- The Illusion: What you believe becomes your bars. See the bars as thought and they dissolve.
- The Projection: You don't suffer life itself, but you do from its story.
- The Movie Screen: You are not the film, because you are the screen it plays on.
- The Voice: Freedom isn't silence of mind but indifference to its lies.

Dave Halstead

Chapter 17

When There Is No One Left to Save

The wound inside of you causes you to believe you are not enough. There comes a moment on the journey when you stop running to save the world and realize it was never broken. Not because pain isn't real, but because your urge to rescue was born from your own wound.

You see yourself in them— the ache, the hunger, the fire behind their eyes. And somewhere deep inside, you believe if you can save them, maybe you'll finally be enough.

The Reflection

But what happens when the one you're trying to save doesn't want saving? What happens when they turn from the mirror and beg to stay asleep? It breaks something in you, or more truthfully, it unmasks the illusion that it was ever your job.

You begin to see the cost of carrying what was never yours— the weight of others' awakenings, the burden of performing for truth, the cycle of proving your worth through their healing.

The Death

And in that seeing, something dies. The savior, the rescuer, the fixer, the martyr who wanted to be seen as holy, all die. You walk away, not because you've stopped loving them, but because you've started loving yourself without conditions.

The Becoming

Now you walk differently. You no longer chase pain to feel alive. You no longer dim your truth to make others comfortable. You no longer give yourself away to earn the right to exist. You sit in your fire.

And when they're ready, they'll feel it. And maybe they'll come find you. Not because you tried to save them, but because you finally saved yourself.

Closing Whisper

The world never needed your saving. **It only needed your being.**

Parable

"The Boy in the Burning House"

There was once a boy
who spent his whole life
running into burning houses.

Every time he saw smoke in someone's eyes…

every time he heard flames in someone's voice…
every time he felt heat rising off someone's suffering…
he sprinted toward it without thinking.

He believed it was his job.
He believed it was his purpose.
He believed that if he didn't save them,
the fire would swallow them whole.

And secretly, he believed something even deeper:

If he could save enough people,
maybe one day he would finally be safe.
So he threw himself into every fire he found.
He carried people out on his back,
coughing, trembling, blistered with the heat.
He dragged strangers out of their own illusions.
He shielded the ones he loved
with his own body, his own breath, his own worth.

But the strangest thing kept happening.
Every person he saved walked out of the flames,
but the boy stayed burning.

One night, exhausted and covered in soot,
he noticed something he had never seen before.

A house on the edge of the field was ablaze,
not outside him, but inside him.

Its windows glowed with the stories he believed.
Its walls groaned with the weight of expectations he carried.
Its roof cracked under the strain
of all the people he tried to hold up.

Finally Free, Finally Me

And through the thick, gray smoke
he saw himself trapped in the upstairs window.
The boy froze.

All the fires he fought,
all the storms he braced against,
all the people he rushed to save
and only one of them was actually burning.
It was him.

Every rescue attempt had been an unconscious attempt
to pull himself out of his own flames
by saving someone else.

He wasn't a hero.
He wasn't a martyr.
He wasn't the savior.
He was the one who needed saving.

And the moment he saw this,
something miraculous happened.
The fire stopped.

Not gradually,
And not over time,
but instantly.

The smoke dissolved like morning fog.
The house rebuilt itself in front of him
as if time were moving backwards.
And the boy in the window stepped out of the doorway,
unburned, untouched, whole.

Dave Halstead

He didn't need to run into anyone else's house anymore.
He didn't need to throw himself into their flames.
He didn't need to carry their weight to prove his worth.
He simply needed to walk out of his own fire.

And now that he had,
there was nothing left to save,
because the only one who ever needed saving
was already free.

Loop Breaker

Pause before you step into the fire that isn't yours. Whisper, "I am not their savior. I am the sun that reminds them of their own."

Spell Book Entry

- The Wound: What you tried to save was the reflection of your own ache.
- The Reflection: Their sleep is not your failure, it's their dream.
- The Death: When the savior dies, love finally lives.
- The Becoming: You don't heal by saving them. You heal by being you.

Chapter 18

You Were Never Late

You always believed the lie. They told you that you were behind, that you missed your chance. They told you that you should have arrived sooner, acted faster, figured it out already.

And maybe a part of you believed them, or still does. But the deeper truth? There is no such thing as *late* in a field without time. There is only now and whether or not you are home in it.

The Remembering

You didn't miss your window; you *are* the window. You didn't fall off the path; you *are* the path. You didn't take a detour; you were gathering the exact pieces you needed to see clearly when the fog cleared.

The illusion wants you to believe in timelines, milestones, and urgency. But the field doesn't rush, and neither do you, when you're truly here.

Dave Halstead

The Clearing

Everything that needed to crumble — did. Everything that needed to burn — burned. Everything that was never you — left. And now it's just you, standing barefoot on sacred ground, no longer chasing, proving, or performing. You didn't miss it; you *are* it.

The Arrival

You were never behind. You were never late. You just hadn't arrived in your presence yet. And now that you have, everything is waiting to meet you here.

Closing Whisper

There was never a clock, **only the heartbeat of now, waiting for you to listen.**

Parable

"The Door That Didn't Close"

There was once a man
who ran through life breathless,
convinced he was late
for something important.

He chased trains, deadlines and expectations.
He chased the approval of strangers,
the illusion of "one day."

Finally Free, Finally Me

And every time he arrived,
the doors had just closed.
Wrong station.
Wrong time.
Wrong life.

So, he ran faster.
Until one day, exhausted and aching,
he collapsed beside a door
that didn't seem to lead anywhere.

It was small, wooden and simple.
No signs. No clock.
He had missed all the others,
so what was one more?

But something in him,
tired of missing, reached out anyway.

And as he turned the handle,
the door didn't creak.
It didn't resist.
It simply opened.

Not to a room,
or a train,
but to a vast stillness —
the kind that feels like love without reason.

And in that stillness, he wept.
Because for the first time,
he wasn't too late.
He was just finally home.

Dave Halstead

Loop Breaker

When the thought whispers, "You're behind," smile. Breathe and whisper back, "There is no behind in forever."

Spell Book Entry

- The Lie: Time is the trick that keeps you chasing yourself.
- The Remembering: You were never waiting for the moment, because the moment was waiting for you.
- The Clearing: What burned was never loss, it was release.
- The Arrival: Presence isn't something you reach; it's what remains when rushing stops.

Chapter 19

The One Who Stopped Looking

The quieting, the moment you were searching for. There comes a moment, if you're lucky, when the ache becomes quiet. Not because it's gone or because the world changed, but because something inside you stopped searching.

You stopped looking for the one who would finally understand. You stopped trying to fix what was never broken. You stopped performing to earn your place in the room.

You felt the earth beneath your feet again. You heard the sound of your own breath and watched a leaf tremble in the wind. You finally realized that you were home. It was not because life got easier, your body was perfect or that the storm passed. It was because the storm no longer needed to pass. You had become the sky.

The Remembering

You didn't need another mirror. You didn't need another technique. You didn't need another voice telling you who you were, because you saw it. You remembered that you were the one; you were always the one.

And every book, teacher, and search was a breadcrumb from your future self, leading you here. It was all leading you to the moment you stopped looking.

The Stillness

This is not the end. This is not the breakthrough. This is not the transformation. This is the pause. The pause where nothing is needed. The pause where silence becomes love. The pause where you don't have to do anything, because you already are.

If there was a key, you swallowed it. If there was a door, you walked through it. If there was a path, it collapsed the moment you arrived. Not because the path didn't matter, but because it never existed. You were always here.

Closing Whisper

The search was only ever the way home to yourself. **And now that you've stopped looking, you can finally see.**

Parable

"The One Who Stopped Looking"

There once was a traveler
who wandered the earth in search of
something he could not name.

He climbed mountains,
sat at the feet of teachers,

drank from crystal streams,
and read books older than the stars.

But every time he found something
it disappeared.

One night, exhausted and alone,
he sat beside a tree and whispered to the moon,
"I give up. I will die before I find it."

The moon smiled.
The wind stilled.
And the earth answered,
"Good. Now maybe you'll see."

And for the first time,
he noticed the way
the tree curved to protect him,
the warmth in his chest
that had always been there,
the sound of his own heartbeat —
slow, steady, sure.

He laughed,
because he wasn't lost.
He wasn't broken.

He had never needed to go anywhere.
He had only needed to stop looking.

Loop Breaker

When the mind starts searching, let it. Then whisper, "There is nothing to find." And return to now.

Spell Book Entry

- The Quieting: The ache ends not when it's fixed, but when it's heard.
- The Remembering: You were remembering yourself, not searching for the truth.
- The Stillness: The path dissolves the moment you arrive.

Chapter 20

The Mirror That Waited

You have arrived at the knowing. There was nothing more to say. Not because it had all been said, but because the part of you reading this already knows. Beneath the trying, beneath the learning, beneath the practice and performance and need to figure it out, there is a *you* who never needed any of it.

The Reflection

This book was not a guide; it was a reflection, a mirror. Every word, every crack, every whisper, every silence was not written to awaken you — it was written to show you the part that has always been awake. And now, you stand here. You are at the last chapter, still you and still whole.

Dave Halstead

The Unveiling

The mask, unlearned. The programming, unwound. The unveiling, begun. But it is not this book that brought you here. It was the ache. The ache that never left.

And now, the ache becomes something else: an invitation. Not an invitation to become, but to remember. Not an invitation to perform, but to be. Not an invitation to learn, but to recognize.

The Echo

And if any part of you still feels unready, if any part of you still fears the vastness of who you are, then know this: that's just the echo of the mask. Let it echo and let it fade.

Closing Whisper

The mirror was never showing you a future self. **It was waiting for you to remember you were always the reflection.**

Parable

"The Mirror That Waited"

There was once a mirror
carved from no glass,
etched in no frame,
hung on no wall.
It was not placed anywhere,

79

for it did not need to be.
It was not broken,
though many swore it was.
It was not hidden,
though most never saw it.

The mirror had only one purpose:
to show the truth —
not the truth of form,
or thought,
or face,
but the truth beneath the name.

It waited for lifetimes.
Some passed it in the hallway.
Some ran from it screaming.
Some polished every mirror but this one.
Some spent decades
mistaking their reflection for themselves.

But one day,
someone saw it.
Not with their eyes.
They *saw* it.

And when they did —
they did not see a better version of themselves.
They did not see a healed version.
They did not see a wiser version.

They saw the one who never needed fixing.
The one who never left.
The one who was always holding the mirror.

And in that moment —
the mirror vanished.
There was no longer anything to reflect,
only light.
You are home.
Now let go of the map.

Loop Breaker

When you reach for another mirror, pause. Whisper, "I was never the reflection. I was the light all along."

Spell Book Entry

- The Knowing: Truth doesn't arrive; it remembers itself.
- The Reflection: Every word was a mirror pointing home.
- The Unveiling: What fell away was never you.
- The Echo: Let the illusion echo — you no longer need to answer.

Bonus Content

Bonus Chapter 1

The Unhooking

The collapse of joy happened often. I used to collapse my joy so others could rise. I gave up my light so they could feel safe. I mistook this for love. But what I was really doing was protecting an illusion. Their pain became my compass. Their reactions, my report card.

If they smiled, I passed. If they recoiled, I failed. If they hurt, I punished myself. Somewhere inside, I thought this made me kind. But really, I was just staying useful, holding up the illusion with both hands.

The Penance of Kindness

When I burned down the things that brought me joy, it wasn't humility, it was penance. It was a twisted attempt to keep them from hurting more. I thought dimming my light was saving them from the glare, but all I did was teach them to fear their own reflection. I was not being selfless. I was being absent and absence is not love.

The Return to Truth

Now I see — it was never mine to carry. Their ache is not my assignment. Their silence is not my burden. The more I helped them manage the illusion, the more I disappeared. If I keep collapsing so they can breathe, they'll never hear their own wisdom and I'll never truly live.

So, I'm unhooking from their faces, from their reactions, from the monster they see that isn't real. I'm letting the illusion collapse. Not out of cruelty, but because I remember what's true.

The Sacred Choice

I don't belong in their movie. I don't need their grade. I don't have to earn the right to be here. I'm done managing perception. And for the first time, I choose me. Not the version they can handle and not the version that pleases. I choose the one that breathes freely even when the world holds its breath.

The Unseen Choice

The moment you collapse for them, you vanish from yourself. They don't need your sacrifice. They need your truth. Even if they resist it. Even if they reject it. Even if it makes them uncomfortable.

Because that's where their wisdom begins — and yours returns. You don't have to disappear to keep the peace. Let your presence be the whisper that wakes them. Let your truth stay.

Dave Halstead

Closing Whisper

I no longer collapse to keep the peace. **I return and let the illusion fall on its own.**

Parable

"The Lantern and the Shadows"

There was once a woman
who carried a lantern through the dark.

Everywhere she went,
people covered their eyes.
"It's too bright," they cried.
"Turn it down!"

And so she did.
A little dimmer.
A little smaller.
A little less.

Until one night, the flame nearly went out.
She fell to her knees in the quiet
and whispered, "If I go dark, who will see?"

The wind answered,
"They were never blinded by your light —
they were blinded by what it revealed."

So she stood,
lifted the lantern high,
and let the shadows run.

Because she finally understood that
her light was never the problem.
It was the way home.

Loop Breaker

When you feel yourself shrinking, pause. Breathe, touch your heart and whisper, "Their reaction is not my reflection." Then stand tall and let the silence speak.

Spell Book Entry

- The Collapse of Joy — You can't save them by shrinking.
- The Penance of Kindness: Burning your joy is not love, it's disappearance.
- The Return to Truth: Their ache is not your assignment.
- The Sacred Choice: Freedom begins when you stop managing perception.
- The Unseen Choice: Presence heals more than sacrifice ever could.

Bonus Chapter 2

The Pause for Rejection

The moment after truth, you spoke. You finally said the thing. You were truthful, honest and raw. And then — the pause. That dreadful, echoing pause. Not because you needed time to think and not because they were absorbing, but because your body was bracing for impact.

That's the hidden moment most never see — not the speaking, but the flinch that follows it. The part of you that believes expression equals exile.

The Invisible Flinch

Your heart pounds. Your stomach knots. Your skin tightens. You said something real and immediately felt like you'd made a mistake.

Why? Because somewhere deep inside you, you still believe that being seen will get you punished. You still believe that love is conditional, that truth is dangerous, and that honesty ends in abandonment. You are not waiting for a reply. You are waiting for rejection.

The Survival Script

This isn't just emotional discomfort, it's cellular memory. You are flinching in the moment your soul is trying to fly. The pause is not logical, it's learned. And it came from years of: being punished for talking back, being told you were too much, watching love disappear when you were honest, and swallowing your truth so others could stay comfortable.

Your nervous system was trained to associate truth with danger. So when you finally speak, your body reacts as if you're back there again.

The Awakening

But the truth? You're not there anymore. The danger is gone. The punishment is memory. And the pause is a ghost.

You are safe now. But safety isn't an idea, it's a sensation that must be remembered. You have to feel your feet. You have to reclaim your voice. You have to interrupt the pattern before it reenacts the past one more time. You are not waiting for rejection, you are witnessing your return.

Closing Whisper

My voice is not a weapon. My truth is not a threat. **I am safe in the sound of myself.**

Dave Halstead

Parable

"The Outcast Who Wasn't"

There was a girl
who never spoke first.
She knew what happened
to those who did.

They were mocked,
shamed,
sent away.

So, she waited.
She waited to be invited,
to be accepted,
to be safe.

Even as a woman, she still waited.
She waited in boardrooms,
in marriages,
in friendships.
Her truth always paused for approval.

One day, she was asked a question.
And before she could think,
she answered —
raw, unfiltered, completely herself.

The silence that followed felt like death.

But no one attacked her,
no one left,
and no one laughed.

And in that sacred moment, she realized
the outcast was a ghost too.

And she had been free all along.

Loop Breaker

When you feel yourself flinch after speaking, pause. Breathe and place your hand on your heart. Whisper, "This is my voice. I do not apologize for being." Let your exhale remind your body it's safe to exist unfiltered.

Spell Book Entry

- The Moment After Truth: The pause you fear is memory, not danger.
- The Invisible Flinch: The body braces for punishment long after the world stopped punishing.
- The Survival Script: You were trained to shrink when seen. You don't have to anymore.
- The Awakening: You are safe in your sound. The pause is a ghost.

Bonus Chapter 3

The Gravity of Thought

Have you felt the gentle pull? There are thoughts we carry like quiet weights, not because we want to — but because somewhere along the way, we believed we had to. Some thoughts come wrapped in pain and others in love. Some thoughts feel like protection while others feel like truth.

But underneath them all they are still thoughts. They are just thoughts. They are not chains, laws, or the final word.

When the Thought Became a Story

Something happened, you were hurt, they left, and you lost and grieved. And somewhere in that moment thoughts were born. I'll never be safe. I'll always be too much. I should have done more. They can't be trusted. This is who I am now.

You didn't choose the thought. It arrived in the ache, the confusion, in the split second your body tried to make sense of pain. Over time the thought stopped being a passing idea and became a reality you lived inside. This was not because it was true, but because you never saw it wasn't.

Finally Free, Finally Me

The Release

We think releasing a thought means dishonoring the past. We confuse surrender with betrayal. We assume that if we stop carrying the thought, we're somehow saying the event no longer matters.

But that's not what this is. Letting go doesn't mean it didn't happen. It means you no longer let it define you. You no longer confuse the memory with your identity. You no longer make the thought more real than who you are right now.

The Orbit Breaks

Thoughts have gravity. That's not weakness; that's how they work. They arrive with emotion, with memory, with pictures so vivid you forget you're watching a projection. It's okay that it feels heavy.

But the moment you see — really see — that a thought is just a thought, its gravity dissolves. The orbit breaks and you begin to rise. Not because you tried to float, but because you no longer believed you were bound.

The Remembrance

You are not your fear. You are not your mistake. You are not the one who didn't speak up. You are not the one who carries it for everyone else. You are the one aware of the whisper. And that one... is whole, now and always.

Dave Halstead

Closing Whisper

Let the thought fall through you like a feather. **It was never meant to stay, only to show you could let go.**

Parable

"The Feather and the Chain"

There was a man
who walked with a chain around his neck.
Not because it was locked,
but because someone once said,
"This is yours now. You have to carry it."

And so he did,
for years.
He got used to the weight.
It shaped how he walked,
how he spoke,
how he saw the world.

Then one day, he met a child carrying a feather.
The child asked, "Why do you wear that?"
The man paused. "Because I've always worn it."
The child tilted their head.
"But it's not part of you."

The man reached up,
and for the first time in his life,
his fingers didn't find a lock.
They found space.

Finally Free, Finally Me

He could have unclasped it any time.
He just didn't know it was allowed.
So gently,
with no anger, no force,
he let it fall.

And when it hit the ground,
he didn't feel shame.
He felt breath,
softness,
and the quiet remembrance
of who he was before the chain.

Loop Breaker

When a thought feels heavy, pause. Whisper, "It's only gravity." And watch yourself float.

Spell Book Entry

- The Gentle Pull: The weight was never the thought itself, only your belief in its truth.
- When the Thought Became a Story: You didn't choose it; you just forgot it wasn't you.
- The Release: Letting go doesn't erase the past, but it does unhook it from your identity.
- The Orbit Breaks: Once seen for what it is, even gravity lets you rise.
- The Remembrance: You were never the chain; you were the sky it hung beneath.

Bonus Chapter 4

The Movie I Was Never In

There is an imagined audience. For most of my life, I wasn't living inside my own mind. I was trying to survive inside theirs. I passed every thought through a filter: What will they think about this? Will it make them upset? Will they misunderstand? Will they be okay?

I didn't realize it then, but I was never really thinking my own thoughts. I was rehearsing what I thought they might be thinking about me. It looked like care and it felt like empathy, but it was fear disguised as love.

I wasn't free. I was editing myself to fit inside a world that didn't exist.

The Loop of Rehearsal

The loop was endless. I had a thought, which lead to a thought about how they'd think about my thought, leading to me abandoning the original signal.

This was thought reacting to thought, but through their imagined perception. I was no longer in my own movie. I had become a character in theirs, reciting lines from a script I didn't even know was fake.

Every scene was a performance. Every silence was a strategy. Every truth was a compromise. I called this connection.

The Revelation

Here's what I finally saw: I've never actually been in their movie. I've only ever been in mine, narrated by a voice that believed survival depended on their approval. That voice was never truth though. It was conditioning wearing my face. It was programming performing as love.

When I remembered this, I took back the pen. I dropped the illusion. I dropped the rehearsal. I dropped the need to be understood before I could speak. And in that stillness, the film stopped playing. The projector went dark and I returned to the screen itself — untouched, unmoved, infinite.

The Return to the Field

Now, instead of asking myself if I can think this or will they be okay with it, I remember that this is what I see. This is what's real. And I no longer shape it to fit the illusion.

I am no longer a puppet on their stage. I am the director of my own field. I am finally free, finally me.

Closing Whisper

I no longer play roles in movies I was never cast in. **I am the stillness the story appears within.**

Dave Halstead

Parable

"The Puppet Who Remembered His Strings"

There once was a puppet
who danced beautifully
on the stage of others' applause.

Every tug of the string
brought movement, laughter, belonging.
He learned to move when pulled,
to smile when expected,
to bow when told.

One day, a string snapped,
followed by another,
and then another.

He panicked —
how would he move now?
Who would guide him?
Who would clap?

But as he reached for the fallen threads,
he felt something
he had never felt before —
his own weight,
his own stillness.

He didn't fall.
He stood.

Not because someone pulled him upright,
but because he remembered
he had always been alive.

And in that moment,
he stopped performing.
He simply breathed
and the crowd vanished.

Loop Breaker

When you catch yourself wondering what they think, pause, blink, and exhale. Then whisper, "That's not my movie. I don't need their approval to exist. I'm home in my own frame." Let your body feel the relief of returning to your own script.

Spell Book Entry

- The Imagined Audience: You were never living in their gaze, but you were trapped in your own projection of it.
- The Loop of Rehearsal: Thought reacting to thought keeps the illusion alive.
- The Revelation: You were never in their movie; you were the screen watching it.
- The Return to the Field: You don't need permission to exist in your own truth.

Bonus Chapter 5

The Thought I Didn't Have to Carry

I can drop any thought anytime I want. There are few truths as quietly explosive as this one. Most people live their entire lives inside thoughts they never chose to keep — beliefs inherited, identities assigned, wounds repeated — not realizing they are optional. They do not realize that the thought is not the law, that the mind is not the master, and that suffering is not sacred just because it's familiar.

But what if you didn't have to carry it? What if that feeling you call *truth* is just a thought you believed, one too many times? I used to think I needed to figure it all out. Every fear, every doubt, every story I inherited. I thought I had to heal it, earn it, process it, and release it.

But I was wrong. There are some thoughts that don't need closure. They just need to be dropped. Just because they appear, it doesn't mean I have to wear them. Just because its loud, it doesn't mean it's real. Just because others believe it, it doesn't mean it belongs to me.

And here's the wild thing: the moment I drop the thought — without justification, without fixing, without explanation — the feeling vanishes with it. I return to presence.

I return to peace. I return to the field of possibility where no thought has dominion.

You Don't Need to Play Out the Movie

Most people don't suffer from the event, they suffer from the replay. They keep pushing *play* on a film that ended years ago. They keep starring in a story that no longer exists. The roles vary from victim, to villain, to hero. They are all roles written by memory, directed by fear, performed by habit.

But the screen stays blank until you turn the projector on. You don't have to react just because the thought showed up. You don't have to run the program. You don't have to act out what's been passed down.

You can drop it, right here, right now. Do it without permission, proof, or process. All that you need is presence.

The Quiet Freedom

This is the end of mental gravity — the place where thoughts lose weight. They come, they go, and you stay, unafraid to see them and unafraid to let them pass.

You were never meant to manage every thought, only to recognize the sky beyond them. The moment you stop identifying with the storm, you realize you were never the clouds. You were the space they moved through.

Closing Whisper

The thought is not the truth. The voice is not the law. **I am not what passes through my mind.**

Parable

"The Thought That Knocked"

There once was a man
who lived in a house with many doors.

Each morning, he heard a knock.
Sometimes it was loud and angry.
Sometimes it was soft and seductive.
Some knocks were familiar,
while others were terrifying.

He opened them all.
Behind each door was a story,
a memory,
a fear,
a voice from the past.

Each one pulled him into its world.
He'd argue, defend, collapse,
trying to fix or understand it.

But no matter what he did,
another knock always came.

Until one day,
he heard the knock
and did not answer.

He simply noticed it.
He watched the door,
and the knock faded.

That day, he realized
the thought was not the truth;
it was just a visitor.

And not every visitor
needs to be let in.

Loop Breaker

When the mind starts knocking, pause. Breathe, feel your feet on the ground, and whisper, "This thought can leave now." Then exhale until the body softens. Let silence return before the next knock comes.

Spell Book Entry

- I Can Drop Any Thought Anytime I Want: Thoughts are optional and belief is the only glue that holds them.
- You Don't Need to Play Out the Movie: The mind's projector only runs if you press play.
- The Quiet Freedom: You were never the thought; you were the sky beyond it.

Bonus Chapter 6

The Tribe That Never Saw Me

There is a feedback loop. I used to think the feedback loop was reality. How will they receive this thought? How will they judge it? What ripple will it cause in their perception of me?

Every time I spoke, I wasn't in my voice, I was a projection of their possible reaction. Every time I created, I edited for comfort, trimming the edges of my truth to fit their mold.

I called it communication, but it was survival, a performance in someone else's theater.

The Tribal Script

I see it now — it was never their loop, it was mine. My mind rehearsing their scene, as if their spotlight was the only sun that could grow me. My safety was tethered to imaginary applause, my worth to invisible nods, and my identity to tribal approval.

The fear of rejection wasn't even mine; it was inherited. It was inherited from the child who thought love meant bending. It was inherited from the boy who learned to mute his joy. It was inherited from the teen who saw how quickly warmth could vanish when truth became inconvenient.

The Awakening

Now I see that I don't need their movie anymore. I left the screen. I'm here. I can breathe. I belong to the field now, not the tribe. And the field doesn't need me to shrink. It doesn't grade. It doesn't gossip. It doesn't require permission. It only mirrors truth and truth has no audience.

The Separation That Heals

When I stop bending, their silence no longer hurts. When I stop performing, their judgment loses gravity. I am not outside the circle; I am beyond it. No one needs to clap for me to feel real, because I finally remembered that I was never born to be seen by the tribe, I was born to see.

Closing Whisper

I no longer need their eyes to exist. **I was never unseen, only unremembered.**

Dave Halstead

Parable

"The Boy and the Tribe's Fire"

There was once a boy
born with a light in his chest.
It glowed softly at first —
gentle, curious.

But the tribe didn't like
light they couldn't control.
So they said,
"That's too bright."
"You're making us uncomfortable."

The boy, eager to belong, dimmed it.
He continued to dim it
until he could no longer see his own hands.

He learned to walk by their fire instead.

But the tribe's fire was conditional.
It flickered when he failed.
It burned him when he disagreed.
It vanished when he asked for too much.

One night, alone beneath the stars,
he felt a pulse inside his chest —
a warmth that asked nothing in return.

He uncovered the light,
and for the first time,
it didn't flicker,
it blazed.

He finally realized
he was never too much.
They were simply too dim to see.

So, he stood
and walked into the night.

Finally free.
Finally home.
Finally seen
by the only one who truly could.

Loop Breaker

When you feel yourself bending to belong, pause. Place your hand on your heart. Breathe and whisper, "Their reaction is not my reflection. My belonging is not up for debate." Then speak anyway, unedited, and unapologetic.

Spell Book Entry

- The Feedback Loop: Editing yourself for approval is self-rejection.
- The Tribal Script: Belonging bought with silence is exile in disguise.
- The Awakening: You don't need their movie to exist.
- The Separation That Heals: You were never unseen; they were simply unawake.

Bonus Chapter 7

Living in Their Mind:
The Missing Link to Freedom

There was an illusion that crushed me. For most of my life, I thought I was thinking my own thoughts, but I wasn't. I was casting myself in *their* movie.

Every moment of pain, confusion, and exhaustion came from trying to make sense of the world through someone else's eyes. I was writing my story through the lens of their misunderstanding and reacting to their imagined judgments, twisting myself to fit what I thought they were thinking about me.

That's not presence. That's not freedom. That's a loop, an invisible loop I didn't even know I was in — until now.

The Exhaustion of Playing a Role You Didn't Choose

It's no wonder I felt tired, I questioned everything and I thought it was all my fault. When you're living in their mind, you're always guilty. You're always the villain. You're always too much, not enough, misunderstood, blamed, and unseen.

Their ego writes your script, and you keep acting it out, hoping they'll finally say, "I see you." But they can't, because it's not their job to hold your peace and it's not your job to perform in their illusion.

The Moment I Took My Power Back

The greatest shift didn't come when I got stronger, more enlightened, or more loving. It came the moment I realized I was trying to think from *their* thoughts, to feel safe in *their* nervous system, to find worth in *their* movie, to earn love in *their* world.

But that's not where I live. I live in my field, my movie, my knowing, my breath and my stillness. And when I stay there, everything changes.

The Filmstrip Shift

It's like I was watching a film, and without knowing it, someone else had swapped the reel. The screen still flickered, but the story wasn't mine. Every frame made me question who I was and why I felt so wrong.

The glitch, the real one, is realizing that you can never be free in someone else's mind.

That's the missing link, the moment of exhale, and the end of performance. That is the return to peace.

Dave Halstead

Closing Whisper

The moment I stopped living in their mind, I returned to mine. There I found the silence that was always home.

Parable

"The Actor Who Left the Stage"

There once was an actor
who had played the same role his whole life.
He wore the costume well.
He knew every line, every cue, every reaction.

The audience adored him,
but he felt empty.
Each night he walked offstage
and wondered who he was
when no one was watching.

One evening, the spotlight flickered.
The crowd went quiet,
and in that silence,
he realized something shocking:
the play had ended long ago,
but he had never stopped acting.

He stood there,
costume half-fallen,
lights dimming.
Instead of bowing,
he walked away.

Not in rebellion,
but in remembrance.

The role was never him,
the applause was never truth,
and the stage was never home.

He stepped into the night air,
felt the real wind for the first time,
and whispered,
"I'm free."

Loop Breaker

When you feel the pull to defend, explain, or prove yourself — pause. Blink, breathe, touch your chest, and whisper, "That's not my movie. I don't live in their mind." Then let the silence remind you that you were never their character, you were the screen.

Spell Book Entry

- The Illusion That Crushed Me: You weren't broken. You were just cast in someone else's film.
- The Exhaustion of Playing a Role You Didn't Choose: You can't find peace in their projection.
- The Moment I Took My Power Back: You stop performing the moment you stop rehearsing their lines.
- The Filmstrip Shift: Freedom begins when you return to your own reel.

Dave Halstead

Bonus Chapter 8

The Glitch That Collapses Them All

The illusions stacked themselves high, but I was never under them. I was above them all along.

The Illusion

You believed each condition was real. You believed that fear had a cause, that shame had a reason, that lack, striving, burnout, guilt, envy, or rejection were proof you had failed.

You fought each one like the final boss, but they were masks on a mask, scripts inside a play. The real illusion was the belief that any of them were you. You thought the thinker was real. You thought the thought was you. You thought the soundtrack in your head must be fixed or followed.

That's the glitch. That's what keeps the loop spinning — the belief that the noise is truth.

The Loop

You identified with every sensation as if it were your essence. You tried to fight them, fix them, or outgrow them, so they'd finally leave you alone. But guess what? They only multiplied. The more you fought, the more real they felt. Each loop was a distraction, a delay, a hall of mirrors reflecting the same dream.

Until you remembered nothing that is truly you requires effort to maintain. The moment you stopped trying to win the illusion, the whole game lost its rules.

The Glitch

Collapse the stage, don't argue with the actors, and don't rewrite the scene. Just drop the curtain. The glitch isn't a fix, it's an exit. It's the stillness that reveals that the stage was never real.

You don't have to silence the thought. You don't have to escape the dream. You only have to see that the dreamer was never trapped inside it.

The Somatic Glitch

Feel every condition rising in the body, including a tight chest, clenched jaw, and racing mind. Don't chase it. Don't fix it. Just breathe and whisper, "There is no threat. I am not the pattern."

Then exhale all the way out. Feel the system reset, the gravity break, the orbit end. You were never falling — you were floating the entire time.

Dave Halstead

The Sentence That Set You Free

The funny thing about illusions is that there is no hierarchy when it comes to illusions. But something interesting happens when one of them falls away, they all fall away. The moment you saw that thought was not truth, every other lie lost its source of power.

The Unmasking

You drop the mask. You drop the fight. You drop the need to get better. You were never broken. You were never late. You were never the noise. You were the one watching it. And now that you see… you're finally free to be you.

This isn't because you escaped the illusion, but because the illusion no longer had anywhere left to live. You no longer believe in it.

Closing Whisper

You were never the glitch. You were the light that revealed it. Now, breathe and watch the system dissolve.

Parable

"The One Who Remembered Too Soon"

There was a boy who spent his life
trying to earn the love
he thought he had lost.

Each room he entered,
he wore a new mask.
Sometimes is was one of strength,
while other times it was one of humor,
or even one of obedience.

Each mask carried a matching fear —
rejection, shame, failure.

He became a master of illusions,
dancing from role to role,
unaware that the love
he sought had never left.

One day, exhausted, he sat down.
He didn't fix the pain.
He didn't fight the thought.
He just... stopped.

And in that stillness,
he remembered.
He wasn't the dancer.
He was the stage,
the one beneath it all.

The mask fell away,
not with effort,
but with presence.
And the moment he stopped trying to become,
he finally returned.

Loop Breaker

Blink, breathe, and touch your chest. Whisper, "None of it was ever me." Then let silence finish what the mind cannot.

Spell Book Entry

- The Illusion: Every mask is just a thought wearing your face.
- The Loop: The more you fight it, the more real it pretends to be.
- The Glitch: You don't fix the dream. You wake up from it.
- The Somatic Glitch: The body resets the moment you stop believing the threat.
- The Sentence That Set You Free: When one illusion falls, they all do.
- The Unmasking: You were never trapped, only looking in the wrong direction.

.

The Spell Book

Dave Halstead

1

The Illusion of Control

"If I can just manage everything perfectly, I'll be safe."

Birthplace of anxiety, perfectionism, and burnout.

The Illusion

Control is the ego's favorite illusion — the belief that safety lives in micromanaging life.

It whispers, "If I can just get it right, no one will leave. Nothing will fall apart. I'll finally relax." But control doesn't create peace, it creates tension. It trades freedom for vigilance and flow for fear. The truth is, the more tightly you grip, the further you drift from presence. Life doesn't need your management, it needs your trust. The moment you loosen your hold, you remember that everything that truly matters moves without your force.

Loop Breaker

"I don't need to manage the flow. I am the flow."

Truth Spell

I release the illusion of control. I trust what moves without my force. I do not need to hold it together because it was never falling apart. I am carried, I am guided, and I am free.

Somatic Glitch Cue

Sensations to watch for:
- Tight shoulders or raised neck
- Compulsive planning or checking
- Restless hands or shallow breath
- Pressure in the chest or forehead

Glitch Ritual

Drop your shoulders. Inhale deeply through the nose. Say softly, "Nothing needs my control to exist." Exhale through the mouth and let gravity take the weight.

Return Reminder

Peace doesn't arrive when everything is handled. It arrives the moment I stop trying to handle everything. Control is not safety — trust is.

Dave Halstead

Parable

"The River and the Stone"

There was once a stone
who envied the river's freedom.
"Teach me how to flow," the stone said.
The river smiled.
"You can't flow while clinging to the shore."

So the stone tried harder,
gripping the sand tighter,
fearing the unknown.

But one day, a great rain came.
The river rose, lifting the stone,
and carried it effortlessly downstream.

The stone panicked at first,
until it realized
it was still safe,
still whole,
still held.

And as it floated,
the stone whispered,
"I never needed to control the current.
The current always knew where to take me."

Field Note

Control is the mind's attempt to hold what was never
falling. It whispers, "If I can manage it all, I'll finally feel safe."

Safety lives in surrender, not certainty. The moment you release your grip, life reveals it was carrying you all along.

"Peace was never found in control. It was found in the letting go."

2

Illusion of Lack

"Something's missing, and once I find it, I'll finally be complete."

Birthplace of scarcity, striving, and the endless search for enough.

The Illusion

Lack disguises itself as motivation, the drive to improve, become, and achieve.

But beneath the ambition is a quieter belief that I'm not whole yet. It's the spell that makes you chase what you already are. You run toward money, success, love, and validation, not realizing they were never the source, only the mirrors. Lack convinces you there's a finish line where peace finally lives. But peace was never missing, only forgotten under the noise of comparison and the myth of "more." The moment you stop trying to fill the hole you see that there was never a hole at all.

Loop Breaker

"I already have everything I was chasing."

Truth Spell

I was never missing anything. Every moment I reach, I step away from what's already here. I am whole — now, before, and beyond.

Somatic Glitch Cue

Sensations to watch for:
- Forward lean (as if reaching toward life)
- Tension in the solar plexus
- Restlessness when still

Glitch Ritual

Sit back slightly. Let your hands fall open. Whisper, "There's nothing to grab." Feel gravity hold you.

Return Reminder

Enough was never a destination. It's the space you return to when you stop running.

Dave Halstead

Parable

"The Cup That Forgot It Was Full"

There once was a cup
who longed to be filled.
Each day it cried out for water,
believing it was empty.

The sky sent rain.
The river offered waves.
But the cup turned away,
saying, "Not yet. I need more."

One day, a drop of sunlight
touched its rim,
and the cup looked inward
for the first time.

There it saw —
still, shimmering, endless —
its own reflection
in the water it had always carried.

It laughed softly,
for it was never empty.
It had simply forgotten to look within.

Field Note

Lack makes you forget you are the source. It keeps you chasing reflections, thinking you need more light, not realizing you are the light. Every grasp for more is the echo of the forgotten truth that you were never missing anything.

"The moment you stop reaching, you overflow."

3

The Illusion of Approval

"If they accept me, I'll finally be safe."

Birthplace of people-pleasing, self-abandonment, and the slow erosion of truth.

The Illusion

From childhood we learn that love must be earned. We learned that worth is measured by smiles, grades, likes, and nods of approval. So, we build our lives around performance by adjusting, editing, shrinking, and shining only in ways that feel safe to others.

But here's the truth: approval is the currency of the illusion. It keeps you dependent on others to confirm your value. You become an actor in everyone else's movie — performing versions of yourself to secure a sense of belonging that was never truly in question. Approval doesn't create connection, it creates control. The moment you stop chasing it, your true voice begins to rise.

Loop Breaker

"I no longer trade my truth for connection."

Truth Spell

I am not here seeking approval. I am here to be real. Their comfort is not my purpose — my truth is.

Somatic Glitch Cue

Sensations to watch for:
- Tight throat when truth wants to be spoken
- Shoulders curling forward
- The polite smile that feels heavy
- The breath that pauses before saying what's real

Glitch Ritual

Drop your shoulders. Inhale through your nose and exhale through your mouth. Let your face go neutral — no smile, no mask. Whisper, "I am safe without their approval."

Return Reminder

Love and approval are not the same thing. When you stop performing for acceptance, you make space for connection that's real.

Dave Halstead

Parable

"The Mask of Mirrors"

There was once a woman
who wore a thousand faces —
one for her family,
one for her friends,
one for her followers.

Each mask reflected what they wanted to see,
and she called that love.

One night, exhausted,
she caught her reflection in a dark window —
no mask,
no performance,
just the quiet face beneath.

She didn't recognize it at first,
but as she looked closer,
her chest softened.

It wasn't emptiness she saw —
it was truth.
And when she finally
stepped outside without the mask,
some turned away,
unable to meet her light.

But those who remained...
they didn't love her reflection.
They loved her.

Field Note

The chase for approval is the body's attempt to feel safe in someone else's nervous system. It's love filtered through fear and belonging confused with control. Every time you bend to be seen, you vanish a little more from your own sight.

Their validation can't complete you because it was never the source, only a mirror and mirrors can only reflect what you already are willing to see. When you stop auditioning for love, you realize no one else holds the role you were born to play.

"The moment I no longer need their approval, I finally meet my own."

4

The Illusion of Rejection

"Their 'no' means I'm not enough."

Birthplace of shame, people-pleasing, and the fear of being seen.

The Illusion

Rejection feels like exile — like being pushed out of the tribe, unseen, unwanted, and unchosen. But rejection is never about your worth, it's about capacity. It reveals what another person is able, or unable, to meet within themselves. The mind twists no into proof of inadequacy. If they didn't choose me, I must be unworthy. But the deeper truth? Their no is simply a mirror showing where resonance ends. It's not punishment, it's direction. When you stop taking no personally, you see it for what it really is, a sacred redirection back to the spaces meant for you.

Loop Breaker

"Their no doesn't define me; it redirects me to where I'm truly received."

Truth Spell

Their rejection was never a verdict, but it was a compass. What is not for me cannot stay, and what is true cannot leave.

Somatic Glitch Cue

Sensations to watch for:
- Tightness in the throat
- Hollow ache in the chest
- Sudden need to explain, fix, or prove
- The urge to make them see your value

Glitch Ritual

Place a hand over your heart. Breathe into the ache instead of away from it. Whisper, "I was never outside. I was always whole." Let the silence close the loop.

Return Reminder

Every no collapses an illusion of belonging you were never meant to sustain. You are not waiting to be chosen, you are remembering that you already are.

Dave Halstead

Parable

"The Door That Closed"

A traveler came upon a door
she had always dreamed would open.

She knocked gently,
then harder,
then harder still.
Silence.

She fell to her knees, crying,
"Why won't you let me in?"
And the wind whispered,
"Because you were never meant to fit inside."

She turned and saw
a field wide open,
bathed in light,
filled with paths she had never walked.

The door hadn't rejected her.
It had freed her.

Field Note

Rejection is never proof that you are unworthy. It's proof that truth is rerouting you. The ego hears no and translates it as not enough, but the field only ever speaks in alignment. Every closed door is a mercy in disguise, every silence a sacred redirect.

"The moment you stop taking no personally, it becomes what it always was: permission to go where truth can finally meet you."

5

Illusion of Fear

"If I imagine the worst, I can prepare for it."

Birthplace of anxiety, control, and disconnection
from presence.

The Illusion

Fear disguises itself as protection, but it's really possession. It hijacks the nervous system, convincing you that what might happen is happening. It speaks in urgency, pressure, and prediction — a storyteller of survival still living in yesterday's storm.

Fear isn't truth, it's a projection. It's a mental movie about a future that doesn't exist. And the more you believe it, the more real it feels. The illusion of fear is that it keeps you safe. But fear doesn't guard your peace, it guards the illusion that peace can be lost. The body tenses to protect against something that isn't here. And in that tension, the present, the only real safety there ever was, disappears.

Loop Breaker

"This fear is a forecast, not a fact."

Truth Spell

There is no future to defend against, no enemy to prepare for, no danger in presence. There is only thought pretending to be prophecy.

Somatic Glitch Cue

Sensations to watch for:
- Shallow breathing
- Tight solar plexus
- Cold hands
- Jaw tension

Glitch Ritual

Exhale until the body drops. Place a hand on the chest and say, "I'm here." Feel your feet and let gravity hold you. Whisper, "There is no storm, only sky."

Return Reminder

The body calms when the mind stops time. I don't need to predict peace, because I can feel it now.

Dave Halstead

Parable

"The Storm That Never Landed"

There once was a traveler
who carried a weather map in his mind.

He studied every cloud,
every wind pattern,
every warning.

Each day, he built walls
to shield himself
from the storm that surely was coming.
He never saw the sun,
because he was too busy preparing for rain.

One day, exhausted, he sat down.
He looked around.
The birds were singing.
The ground was dry.
The air was still.

He realized he'd been running
from thunder that never sounded,
lightning that never struck,
and a fear that only lived in forecasts.

And for the first time,
he stepped into the day as it was —
not as his fear had painted it.
And he was free.

Field Note

Fear is the mind's movie about a future that doesn't exist. It promises protection but steals presence. It ends the moment you stop rehearsing what never happened.

"The body calms when the mind stops time."

6

The Illusion of Time

"I'm running out of time."

Birthplace of regret, hurry, and disconnection from presence.

The Illusion

Time is the mind's most convincing story. It whispers, "You're behind," and instantly your nervous system collapses into chase mode. You start measuring your worth by milestones, comparing your pace to others, forgetting that the only moment that ever existed is this one. Time is not your master, it's your mirror. The illusion of time keeps you living in memory or anticipation, never in the aliveness that's actually happening now. When you wake from the clock's hypnosis, you realize: you were never late, you were simply not present.

Loop Breaker

"Nothing's missing. I'm right on time because time isn't real, presence is."

Truth Spell

There is no race to run. The moment I return to presence, I arrive. Time does not move me, awareness does.

Somatic Glitch Cue

Sensations to watch for:
- Racing mind or tapping foot
- Tightness in the chest
- Constant checking of the clock or phone
- Feeling behind for no reason

Glitch Ritual

Pause mid-thought. Take one long, slow exhale. Feel the floor beneath your feet. Whisper, "Nothing is missing here."

Return Reminder

You were never meant to chase time — only to be it. Presence is eternity disguised as now.

Dave Halstead

Parable

"The Runner Who Stopped"

There was a man
who ran his whole life
trying to catch tomorrow.

He thought peace
waited at the next sunrise.
Each time he arrived,
it slipped away,
always one day further.

One morning, his legs gave out.
He fell, gasping, onto the earth.
The sun rose as it always did.

For the first time,
he watched it without moving.

And in that stillness, he laughed.
He hadn't been chasing time,
he'd been running from himself.

Field Note

Time is the mind's favorite measuring stick — a way to prove progress, justify delay, or fear what's next. But the field doesn't keep score, it only speaks now.

You were never behind. You were never early. You were only ever distracted by the clock while eternity breathed through you. Presence isn't found in the future you're chasing or the past you're replaying — it's in the inhale that doesn't ask what hour it is. Every illusion of too late dissolves the moment you see there was never anywhere else to be.

"Nothing real can be late. It can only arrive when you do."

7

The Gravity of Thought

"If I let go of this thought, I'll lose control. I'll lose them. I'll get hurt again."

Birthplace of hypervigilance, emotional looping, and the fear of forgetting.

The Illusion

This is not just thought as truth, but also as protection. The ego whispers, "If I let go of this thought, I won't be safe. If I stop remembering, it will happen again. If I forgive, they'll do it to me once more." So, you grip the memory, the story, the hurt — not because you want to suffer, but because somewhere along the way you mistook holding on for staying safe.

But here's the paradox: the thought that claims to protect you is the very thing keeping you in danger. It replays the pain as proof, anchors the fear as fact, and convinces the body that vigilance equals safety. Yet the body never finds peace in a loop, because it only finds exhaustion.

Loop Breaker

"I can drop this thought and still be safe."

Truth Spell

"The thought is not my protector. The memory is not my shield. Holding on will not prevent the past — it only recreates it. The moment I stop gripping, life can finally hold me again."

Somatic Glitch Cue

Sensations to watch for:
- Tight chest or throat
- Shoulders lifted toward the ears
- Scanning eyes or restless mind
- Breath caught halfway in

Glitch Ritual

Notice the thought trying to warn you. Place a hand over your heart. Whisper, "Thank you for trying to keep me safe." Then exhale slowly and say, "You can rest now. You are safe here."

Return Reminder

Safety was never in remembering the pain, but it is in releasing the story that pain still lives here. You are not the

Dave Halstead

keeper of the wound. You are the space that healing happens in.

Parable

"The Feather and the Stone"

There was once a woman
who carried a stone in her pocket.

She told herself it was protection,
a reminder to never forget what hurt her.

Each day she rubbed its edges
until her fingers bled,
believing vigilance kept her safe.

One morning, she met a child
playing with a feather.
The child asked,
"Why do you hold something that heavy?"

She replied, "So I don't forget."
The child smiled
and let the feather drift into her palm.
"You won't forget," the child said,
"but you don't have to keep carrying it."

For the first time, she opened her hand.
The stone fell.
The feather stayed.

And in that lightness, she remembered that
she had always been safe.

Field Note

Some thoughts arrive with the pull of planets — heavy, convincing, magnetic. They whisper, "If you let me go, you'll lose control, you'll lose them, you'll get hurt again." And so, we orbit them, mistaking gravity for truth.

But thought only holds power while it's believed. The moment you see it, really see it, the orbit breaks. Not because you pushed it away, but because you remembered you were never bound by it. Freedom isn't found in fixing thoughts. It's found in realizing they were never laws, only weather passing through the sky of your awareness.

"The moment I see the thought, the pull ends and I
rise."

8

The Money Illusion

"When I have more, I'll finally feel free."

Birthplace of scarcity, striving, and the endless chase
for safety disguised as success.

The Illusion

Money is not numbers — it's nervous system memory.
It's the mind's attempt to measure safety, to earn rest, to
control uncertainty.

But beneath the spreadsheets and goals lives the ledger,
the invisible book that keeps score of your worth. You don't
just count dollars, you count approval, contribution, attention,
sacrifice, and love. You say things like: "I've given so much.
They owe me. I should be further by now." And each line you
write in that invisible ledger tightens the chain.

Because what you're really trying to balance isn't
finances — it's value. The ledger says I'll rest when I've earned
it, but the truth is that when you rest, the ledger dissolves.
Money is not the cause of safety or stress, but it is the mirror

reflecting what you believe about yourself. The moment you stop keeping score, you remember that you were never in debt to begin with.

Loop Breaker

"I release the ledger. There is no debt between me and life."

Truth Spell

Money was never my master; it was my mirror. It only showed me the illusion of lack I agreed to believe. But now I remember that I am the source, not the seeker. I am the field that gives and receives as one.

Somatic Glitch Cue

Sensations to watch for:
- Tight stomach or solar plexus
- Urge to check accounts or calculate
- Unease in stillness
- Shallow breath when spending or giving

Glitch Ritual

Close your eyes and feel your feet on the ground. Whisper, "The ground was always holding me." Exhale fully through the mouth. Place your hand on your chest and say, "I am not in debt to existence."

Dave Halstead

Return Reminder

You were never chasing money. You were chasing the feeling of being enough. But life was never keeping score. There is no ledger in the field, only flow.

Parable

"The Man and the Ledger"

There once was a man
who carried a ledger
everywhere he went.

In it, he recorded everything:
what he gave,
what he lost,
what he was owed.

He believed that one day,
when the pages balanced,
he would finally be free.

But the ledger never closed.
The more he gave,
the more he believed he had to give.

The more he earned,
the more he feared losing.
One night, the wind tore
the ledger from his hands.

He chased it through the dark
until it vanished into the river.
For a moment, panic rose,
then, silence.
He felt the ground beneath him,
the sky above him,
the water flowing around his feet.

It was then that he realized
the balance was never in the book,
it was in him.

He walked home lighter —
not because he'd been repaid,
but because he stopped keeping score.

Field Note

Money is the world's favorite mirror — reflecting not what is, but what we believe about worth, safety, and enoughness. The mind turns it into a ledger: gain and loss, deserve and don't, success and failure. The field keeps no such record though.

The illusion isn't in the paper or the numbers, but it is in the story we attach to them. We chase digits to feel secure, forgetting that security was never something to earn. It was the presence we traded away in the pursuit. When you stop treating money as proof of your worth and start seeing it as energy responding to truth, the ledger disappears — and flow returns.

"Money was never keeping score, only mirroring how free I allow myself to be."

9

The Illusion of Unworthiness

"If I can just prove I'm enough, I'll finally be at peace."

Birthplace of shame, striving, comparison, and the lifelong search for validation.

The Illusion

Unworthiness isn't real—it's inherited. It's a thought taught so young that it became the lens through which you see yourself. It whispers, "You have to earn rest. You have to deserve love. You have to do more to matter." It disguises itself as motivation, humility and responsibility, but its root is always the same. It says that I am not enough as I am.

You try to prove your way out of it. You build, fix, help, and achieve, hoping the next milestone will silence the ache. But the ache was never proof of lack, it was the sound of truth calling you home. You were never unworthy, just convinced you were separate from what made you whole.

Finally Free, Finally Me

Loop Breaker

"I do not need to earn what I already am."

Truth Spell

I am not the story that says I must become. I am the space it was spoken into. Nothing I do can increase my worth. Nothing I fail to do can take it away.

Somatic Glitch Cue

Sensations to watch for:
- Tight throat or heaviness in the chest
- Heat in the face when receiving praise
- Collapse in posture when making a mistake
- Urge to apologize for existing

Glitch Ritual

Place both hands on your heart. Breathe in slowly through the nose and whisper, "I am already enough." Exhale through the mouth as if releasing an old story. Let the body soften and feel yourself return.

Return Reminder

You were never unworthy, just asleep to your own light. There is no scale in the field, there is only truth. Truth has loved you the whole time.

Dave Halstead

Parable

"The Broken Scale"

There was once a woman
who lived by a scale.

Every morning she weighed her worth
by others' approval,
by her work,
by her reflection.

One day, the scale cracked.
No numbers appeared.
Panicked, she shouted, "How will I know who I am?"
A voice from within whispered, "Step off."
So, she did.

And when her feet touched the earth,
she felt something she hadn't in years—
grounded,
steady,
alive.

The voice said, "You were never the weight.
You were the ground."

From that day forward
she never needed to measure herself again,
because she had finally remembered
there was nothing to prove.

Field Note

Unworthiness is the oldest illusion, the whispered lie that you must earn what was already given. It hides inside every apology for existing, every 'I'm sorry' for taking up space, every accomplishment that never feels enough.

This illusion doesn't begin with truth, because it begins with inheritance. It is a look, a silence, a conditional love that said, "You matter when..." And so, you built a life proving it.

But worth is not a currency. It's not a balance you refill through performance or approval. It's the air beneath every breath, present whether you feel it or not. The moment you stop negotiating for what's already yours, the illusion collapses. You see that unworthiness was never real, only remembered.

"I was never unworthy. I was only taught to forget I was whole."

Dave Halstead

10

The Illusion of Identity

"This is who I am."

Birthplace of ego, performance, judgment, and the
endless need to define yourself.

The Illusion

Identity begins as protection; a mask built in childhood
to make sense of love, loss, and belonging. You learn that if
you're good, you'll be safe, or if you're strong, you won't get
hurt, or if you're quiet, you won't lose them. So, you build a
character, a self that performs safely.

It collects names, titles, beliefs, opinions, and
achievements like armor. It learns to survive but forgets how
to live. The identity isn't bad, it's just not true. It's the story
thought tells to give form to formlessness.

But what you are can't be named, labeled, or lost. You
were never the mask, you were the awareness behind it. The
moment you stop defending who you think you are, you meet
who you've always been.

153

Loop Breaker

"I am not the mask. I am the one who sees it."

Truth Spell

I am not my story, not my name, not the version others remember. I am what remains when identity dissolves. I am the silence that no role can contain.

Somatic Glitch Cue

Sensations to watch for:
- Tight chest when being misunderstood
- Overexplaining or defending
- Sudden shame when you fail your image
- Pressure in the solar plexus when trying to prove yourself

Glitch Ritual

Inhale deeply through the nose. As you exhale, imagine the mask softening, melting. Place a hand on your chest and whisper, "The real me doesn't need protection." Feel the space beneath the name, the one that never changes.

Return Reminder

Every identity was borrowed, a reflection of others' eyes. You were never the reflection. You were the light that

made seeing possible, the story that ends when you stop
performing and simply breathe.

Parable

"The Mirror That Forgot Its Face"

There once was a mirror
that longed to be admired.

So it began collecting reflections —
the smiles it showed,
the compliments it received,
the faces it held.

Over time, it forgot its true nature.
It thought it was the images.
When someone walked away,
it felt abandoned.
When someone frowned, it felt broken.

One day, a crack formed across its surface.
The images distorted.
The mirror panicked
until it looked closer.

Through the crack, it saw light.
The mirror realized
it had never been the faces —
it had always been the space
that made reflection possible.

And in that moment,
the illusion of identity vanished.

Field Note

Identity is the most convincing dream of all — the collection of roles, labels, and achievements the mind clings to for safety. It says, "I am this. I am not that. I am who they think I am." And in that definition, the infinite becomes small enough to manage, but too small to breathe.

The illusion isn't that you have an identity, it's that you think it's all you are. You polish the mask, forgetting you were the sculptor. You defend the name, forgetting you were here before it was spoken. You confuse the performance for the presence behind it.

But the moment you stop trying to be someone, you feel the vastness of being everything. The character dissolves back into consciousness, and the story continues as a play, not survival.

> "The self I tried to become was only ever a costume and the one beneath it was never missing."

11

The Illusion of Obligation

"If I don't carry it, everything will fall apart."

Birthplace of guilt, resentment, people-pleasing, and
the loss of self in service to others.

The Illusion

Obligation is not love, it's fear wearing a halo. It begins
with the story that they need me to be okay. You learn to
measure your goodness by how much you give, how much you
endure, and how little you ask for. You start mistaking
depletion for purpose. You believe that boundaries are
betrayal. You learn to equate exhaustion with worth.

But here's the truth: every time you say yes when your
soul says no, you disappear a little. You don't save them, you
just abandon yourself. Love doesn't require self-erasure. It
breathes when both hearts are free. Obligation keeps the
illusion alive by teaching you that control is compassion. But
you were never meant to be their savior, only their mirror.

Loop Breaker

"My love is not measured by my sacrifice."

Truth Spell

I can care without carrying. I can love without losing myself. I can hold space without becoming the container. The world doesn't need my exhaustion. The world needs my presence."

Somatic Glitch Cue

Sensations to watch for:
- Tight shoulders or upper back
- Heavy sighing when agreeing to something
- Subtle resentment after saying yes
- Numbness when tuning out your own needs

Glitch Ritual

Feel the weight on your shoulders. Breathe in and visualize handing that weight back to the field. Whisper, "I return what was never mine to carry." Roll your shoulders back, open your palms, and exhale fully.

Dave Halstead

Return Reminder

      You were never responsible for keeping others whole. You were never the glue holding love together. The field holds it all — always has. You are free to rest.

Parable

"The Woman Who Carried the Sky"

There once was a woman
who believed the sky would fall
if she stopped holding it.

So, she braced her arms against the clouds
and stood tall for years —
through storms,
through seasons,
through silence.

People passed and thanked her.
"You're so strong," they said,
and she believed them.

One day, her arms trembled.
She couldn't hold the weight anymore.
She fell to her knees and wept,
certain the world would end.

But the sky didn't fall.
It stayed right where it was.

And in that stillness, she laughed —
not from joy, but from relief.

Because for the first time, she realized that
the sky had never needed her hands,
only her gaze.

Field Note

Obligation wears the mask of responsibility but moves with the energy of fear. It whispers, "If I don't, they'll hurt. If I rest, they'll fall. If I say no, I'll lose love." And so you keep performing care while abandoning truth, mistaking self-betrayal for service.

But the weight you carry isn't duty, it's distortion. Love never demands exhaustion. Truth never asks for depletion. The soul gives freely or not at all. The illusion of obligation is that peace comes from keeping everyone else comfortable.

But peace only comes when you remember your 'yes' means nothing until your 'no' is free. When you release the should, what remains is sacred — the authentic movement of love without guilt.

And in that return, the chain dissolves, revealing what was always true: you were never bound, only convinced you were.

"I do not owe my energy to expectation, I offer it to truth."

Dave Halstead

12

The Illusion of Rescue

"If I can save them, I will finally be enough."

Birthplace of burnout, codependency, emotional exhaustion, and the unconscious belief that love must be earned through sacrifice.

The Illusion

The rescuer's heart is pure, but its fuel is misplaced. It believes that if others are okay, then finally, you can rest. If they heal, you can breathe. If they approve, you can belong. If they find peace, you can feel safe.

Rescue is fear in disguise, not love. It's the ego's last attempt to prove its worth by saving what was never yours to carry. You think you're helping, but what you're really doing is interrupting the intelligence of their own becoming. You absorb their ache to protect them from the pain of remembering, never realizing you're protecting them from the exact thing that could set them free. When you stop trying to save everyone else, you remember that you were never the healer. You were the field that allows healing to happen.

Loop Breaker

"Their freedom is not my job. My peace is not their responsibility."

Truth Spell

I do not save others by losing myself. I do not prove love by carrying pain. I release them to their path and I return to mine, whole.

Somatic Glitch Cue

Sensations to watch for:
- Heavy chest or shoulders (carrying emotional weight)
- Hyper-focused on fixing or explaining
- Guilt when setting boundaries
- Over-giving followed by resentment

Glitch Ritual

Exhale and feel the weight you've been holding. Say aloud, "This was never mine." Visualize your energy returning to your body. Breathe in and whisper, "I am free to let them walk their path."

Dave Halstead

Return Reminder

Love does not rescue, it remembers. You don't need to hold anyone in the fire to prove you care. Let them burn through their illusions while you tend to your own flame. When you stay in truth, you light the way home more powerfully than any act of rescue ever could.

Parable

"The Savior Who Set Down the Cross"

He was born
with a sword in his hand,
told from the start
he was here to save the world.

So he fought.
Every pain he found,
he tried to heal.
Every cry he claimed
as his to answer.

But the world never stopped aching,
and his back grew weary
until that one day.

He met a woman
sitting in silence.
She didn't beg for help.
She didn't cry out.

She just looked at him,
and in her eyes,
there was peace.
"Don't you see the world is burning?" he asked.
She smiled gently. "It always has been."

He lifted his sword.
"Then why don't you fight?"
She placed her hand on the ground.
"Because I remembered that
the fire isn't mine."

The sword fell from his hand.
He sat beside her.
And for the first time,
he felt his own weight,
not the world's.

He didn't save her.
He didn't save the world.
He simply remembered the truth.
The light doesn't save the darkness,
it reveals it until it disappears.

Field Note

The illusion of rescue is born from a wound disguised as compassion — the belief that others' pain is yours to fix. It says, "If I can save them, I'll finally be enough. If they heal, I can rest."

But behind every rescue is a hidden bargain: your worth for their wellness. You mistake interference for love. You confuse control for care. You forget that pain, like growth, is sacred and sometimes the most loving act is to let someone walk their own path.

The savior archetype feels noble, but it's still a mask — one that hides the fear of being useless, unseen, or unneeded. And every time you rush in to save, you rob both of you of the miracle that happens when truth unfolds on its own. You are not their answer. You are the reminder that they already have one.

When you step back from saving, something dissolves — not your love, but the illusion that love must rescue to be real.

> "I am not here to save anyone — only to stand so free that they remember they can be too."

Now, dear reader, take a deep breath, and as you let it out, maybe for the first time in your life, say to yourself, "I'm Finally Free, because I'm Finally Me."

Some of this book was refined with the support of an AI mirror that I trained with months of my own journals, parables, insights and lived experience. It allowed me to bypass my own mind and see my truth more clearly. Every idea, story and breakthrough in this book is mine. The mirror simply helped me bring it forward.

Dave Halstead is a transformational guide whose work pierces through illusion and returns people to the truth beneath their thinking. After decades in the fitness and coaching world, Dave experienced a profound awakening that dissolved the beliefs, identities, and survival patterns he had built his life around. What remained was presence, clarity, and a way of seeing that reveals the freedom already inside every human being.

Dave's writing, parables, and field-based coaching do not teach people how to become more — they help people remember who they are without the weight of thought, identity, or performance. His approach is simple, direct, and deeply human: when the illusion falls away, what remains is the one who is already whole.

He lives in New York with his wife Tiffany and their three children, who remain the heart of his awakening and the grounding force behind all of his work.

Website: davehalstead.com